GUIDE TO MILITARY CAREERS

ROBERT E. DUNBAR

GUIDE TO MILITARY CAREERS

FRANKLIN WATTS
NEW YORK CHICAGO LONDON TORONTO SYDNEY

355
D899g
c-1
ccL
5/93
18.43

Photographs copyright ©: U.S. Air Force: pp. 2, 27, 47, 113, 122; U.S. Navy: pp. 25, 34, 41, 42, 121; U.S. Army: pp. 33, 45, 50, 54 top, 55, 87, 114, 117; U.S. Marines: p. 40; AP/Wide World Photos: pp. 11, 29, 54 bottom; Monkmeyer Press Photos: pp. 14 (Rogers), 67 (Paul Conklin), 74 top (Spencer Grant); Arms Communications/William B. Folsom: p. 23; Photo Researchers, Inc.: pp.74 bottom (Bettye Lane), 75 (M.E. Warren), 96 (Spencer Grant); Actuality Inc./Polly Brown: p. 78; Gamma-Liaison/ Leif Skoogfors: p. 82.

Library of Congress Cataloging-in-Publication Data

Dunbar, Robert E., 1926-
Guide to military careers/by Robert E. Dunbar.
p. cm.
Includes bibliographical references and index.
Summary: Discusses various aspects of choosing a career in the military, including advantages and realities of military life, choosing which branch to join, and benefits and training.
ISBN 0-531-11118-0
1. United States—Armed Forces—Vocational guidance—Juvenile literature. [1. United States—Armed Forces—Vocational guidance. 2. Vocational guidance.] I. Title.
UB147.D78 1992
355'.0023'73—dc20   92-10921 CIP AC

Copyright © 1992 by Robert E. Dunbar
All rights reserved
Printed in the United States of America
5 4 3 2 1

CONTENTS

ONE   What the Military Can Offer You   9
Financial Help for College/ The Nation's Largest Employer/ Benefits to an Enlisted Person/Personal and Technical Skills/ Opportunities for Education/ Benefits to an Officer/ Education Is Crucial

TWO   Choosing a Branch of Military Service   22
The Army/ The Navy/ The Air Force/ The Marine Corps/ The Coast Guard/ The Armed Services Vocational Aptitude Battery (ASVAB) Test

THREE   Signing On With Uncle Sam   37
Choosing a Job/ Specialty: Medical Laboratory Technician/ Specialty: Audiovisual Production/ Specialty: Computer Systems Analyst/ Specialty: Engine Mechanic/ Combat Specialty: Infantryman

FOUR   Training, Benefits, and Opportunities   53
             for Advancement
Women in the Military/ Pay and Benefits/ The GI Bill/ Financial Incentives/ Allowances for Off-Base Living/ Army Training/ Navy Training/ Air Force Training/ Marine Corps Training/ Coast Guard Training

FIVE   Making the Grade as an Officer   71
Applying to Military Academies/ Officer Training While in College (ROTC)/ After Graduation from College/ Direct Appointments for Professionals and Opportunities for Enlistees/ Training in a Career Specialty/ Continuing Education/ Duty Assignments/ Pay and Benefits/ Retirement and Veterans Benefits/ Choosing a Profession/ Specialty: Purchasing and Contract Manager/ Specialty: Social Worker/ Specialty: Air Traffic Control Manager/ Specialty: Life Scientist/ Specialty: Missile System Officer

SIX   Facing the Realities of Military Life   95
Adjustments Can Be Challenging/ The Married Enlisted Man/ Some Drawbacks from an Officer's Point of View/ From Military to Civilian Life

APPENDIX A: Sample ASVAB Test Questions   103

APPENDIX B: Specialties for Enlisted Men and Women   110

APPENDIX C: Specialties for Officers   119

FOR FURTHER READING   125

INDEX   126

GUIDE TO MILITARY CAREERS

WHAT THE MILITARY CAN OFFER YOU

ONE

Whichever path you decide to take in choosing a job or profession that best suits your abilities and skills, one option worth considering is to find out what the military can offer you. The military option has substantial benefits, whether you join as an enlisted man or woman or meet the qualifications to become commissioned as an officer. In the military the enlisted personnel work in jobs that are equivalent to blue-collar or white-collar jobs in civilian life. Advancement is possible, based on promotions in rank or rating, to the middle management level. Officers in the military are equivalent to various stages of civilian management from junior to senior executives up to the top management level. A general or admiral, for example, is equivalent to the chief executive officer in a large corporation.

★ FINANCIAL HELP FOR COLLEGE ★

Even if you do not want to make a career out of military service, you might want to consider serving for a limited time if you need financial help to realize your ambitions and need opportunities to attend college or professional schools. Serving in the military will make it possible for you to qualify for up to $25,200 if you enlist for four years. Also, there are many opportunities for you to earn credits toward a college degree, with most of your tuition costs paid, while serving in the military. Details on educational and other benefits are described in chapters that follow.

Military recruitment literature strongly emphasizes the fact that in many respects serving in the military is like having a job in civilian life, although there are very distinct and restrictive differences. The typical workday is eight hours, 8:00 a.m. to 5:00 p.m., with time off for lunch. Soldiers often have physical training before normal duty, in which case your day could begin at 6:00 a.m. Your evenings and weekends are free except for those times when you "have the duty," work for someone who is ill, or there is an emergency of some kind. You are paid twice a month and have a thirty-day vacation period each year. However, while serving in the military you are paid on a twenty-four-hour, seven-days-a-week basis, even though you work an eight-hour day, five days a week, under normal conditions. Technically you are on call twenty-four hours a day, so you can respond to emergencies, for example. Also, unlike working at a civilian job, you can't quit before your obligation is completed.

☆ THE NATION'S LARGEST EMPLOYER ☆

When all five branches of the military—Army, Navy, Air Force, Marine Corps, and Coast Guard—are taken into account, the military is the nation's largest employer, with about one and a half million enlisted men and women in its ranks. There are over 2,000 job specialties to choose from, so it should not be difficult to find one that can meet your preferences and expectations. Beginning in 1991, in response to budget re-

A U.S. Special Forces trooper searches house-to-house for Iraqi soldiers in Kuwait City, during Operation Desert Storm. The Special Forces is a branch of the Army.

straints, the military began reducing its forces by about 20 percent, although remaining of formidable size. Each year there are places for about 240,000 enlisted men and women and 20,000 officers, who are needed to replace those who have fulfilled their commitments and returned to civilian life. These needs are met because of the many benefits of military service, for both enlisted personnel and officers, as summarized below.

Benefits of Military Service

★ Money for college, professional, or technical schools
★ Training and experience in skills you can use in civilian jobs
★ Good pay, comparable to similar jobs in civilian life
★ Full medical, dental, and other health care
★ Steady advancement to more responsible positions and higher pay, based on performance, training, and educational requirements
★ Job security, as long as you perform up to military standards
★ Opportunities for education
★ Opportunities for travel

★ BENEFITS TO AN ENLISTED PERSON ★

These are some of the attractions that convinced Marshall Griffin to take the military option. He began military service four months after graduating from high school in 1984. In early 1991, when the war in the Persian Gulf known as Operation Desert Storm was about to begin, he had been put on two-week alert for relocation from his post in Alaska. He was later reassigned to Fort Gordon in Georgia.

After more than six years' service, Sergeant Grif-

PAY GRADE	ARMY	NAVY	AIR FORCE	MARINE CORPS	COAST GUARD
E-9	COMMAND SERGEANT MAJOR / SERGEANT MAJOR	MASTER CHIEF PETTY OFFICER	CHIEF MASTER SERGEANT	SERGEANT MAJOR / MASTER GUNNERY SERGEANT	MASTER CHIEF PETTY OFFICER
E-8	FIRST SERGEANT / MASTER SERGEANT	SENIOR CHIEF PETTY OFFICER	SENIOR MASTER SERGEANT	FIRST SERGEANT / MASTER SERGEANT	SENIOR CHIEF PETTY OFFICER
E-7	SERGEANT FIRST CLASS	CHIEF PETTY OFFICER	MASTER SERGEANT	GUNNERY SERGEANT	CHIEF PETTY OFFICER
E-6	STAFF SERGEANT	PETTY OFFICER FIRST CLASS	TECHNICAL SERGEANT	STAFF SERGEANT	PETTY OFFICER FIRST CLASS
E-5	SERGEANT	PETTY OFFICER SECOND CLASS	STAFF SERGEANT	SERGEANT	PETTY OFFICER SECOND CLASS
E-4	CORPORAL / SPECIALIST 4	PETTY OFFICER THIRD CLASS	SERGEANT / SENIOR AIRMAN	CORPORAL	PETTY OFFICER THIRD CLASS
E-3	PRIVATE FIRST CLASS	SEAMAN	AIRMAN FIRST CLASS	LANCE CORPORAL	FIREMAN / SEAMAN
E-2	PRIVATE	SEAMAN APPRENTICE	AIRMAN	PRIVATE FIRST CLASS	FIREMAN APPRENTICE / SEAMAN APPRENTICE
E-1	No Insignia PRIVATE	SEAMAN RECRUIT	No Insignia AIRMAN BASIC	No Insignia PRIVATE	SEAMAN RECRUIT

Figure 1. Enlisted insignia of the United States armed forces

fin expresses a generally positive attitude about his military experience. He says, "I enlisted in the Army on October 24, 1984, the day after my birthday. At the time I was not sure about college. I had made several choices but wasn't thinking seriously about them." When he joined the Army he expressed interest in training in a radio and television specialty, "but nothing in that career field was open then. So I opted for being a tactical satellite microwave systems operator, a military occupational specialty [MOS]. This job involved training and field experience with the operation of satellite, microwave (superhigh frequency), and tropospheric scatter equipment. The advantages were free training and experience on this equipment *and* travel." He took his basic training at Fort Jackson, South Carolina, and the advanced individual training for his MOS at Fort Gordon. His first overseas assignment was in West Germany.

★ PERSONAL AND TECHNICAL SKILLS ★

One of the most satisfying results of Sergeant Griffin's Army service has been the skills he has learned. "Probably the most important skill I've learned is how to communicate and work with other people. You meet people from all places and walks of life. I have a buddy from my basic training days who still keeps in touch. He's from Guam. We were able to get together when I was stationed in Texas.

"I've learned how to be decisive. It's difficult mak-

(Left) A second-year engineering student at the
New York State Maritime College checks the packing
on a steam valve aboard the SS *Empire State*.

ing decisions, especially when they affect other people's lives, sometimes in a bad way. For example, I had to recommend that one of my soldiers be discharged. He had a bad problem with debt and couldn't get along with others. I knew I had done the best I could to help him, but you have to learn how to weigh both sides—what is good for the soldier as an individual compared to what is good for the group as a whole."

One of the technical skills Griffin has learned is how to operate satellite, tropospheric, and microwave equipment. This skill has its civilian counterpart. "GTE [General Telephone and Electronics Corporation] is a big hirer of those getting out of the service with my MOS from what I hear."

Another important skill he has learned is how to survive on his own. "Tactically, I know how to survive in the wilderness, how to use a magnetic compass, how to orient a map to where I am on the ground, how to build a shelter, etc.—all the survival techniques, including first aid. Alaska is a *great* assignment if you really want to learn how to live off the land."

★ OPPORTUNITIES FOR EDUCATION ★

One of the things Griffin likes best about being in the military is the opportunities for education while in service and when you leave the service. "Education is a *big* plus. The Army will pay 75 percent of the tab if you take college courses while on active duty. There is also the GI Bill. You pay $100 a month for twelve months and the Army will give you a total of $10,800 for college. Military education is also a plus. Many of the military courses and training can be converted to civilian college credits." Enlisted personnel are encouraged to take advantage of educational opportunities, and whatever courses and training they take are noted when they are being considered for promotions.

Griffin says, "Military and civilian schooling will give you points toward promotion, such as for pay grades E-5 and E-6, sergeant and staff sergeant." Though not "education" in the strictest sense of the word, travel has its educational aspects and can bring pleasure. "Travel in the service is *great*," he says. "I was in Germany from April 1985 through October 1987. I loved it. I got to see a lot of Europe. Special travel packages designed for servicemen make travel inexpensive.

"There are a lot of schools, both military and civilian, that you can take advantage of while you're in the service. The more schooling, the better the chance of promotion to the next higher grade. I made Honor Graduate in 1985 from my first Advanced Individual Training (AIT) course. I received promotion from E-1 to E-2 [from first to the next higher grade, in this case, private] early because of that. You can do really well in the military by just applying yourself.

"An excellent school that I had a chance to attend was the electronic journalism school at Fort Benjamin Harrison, Indiana. Everything is taught, from radio broadcasting to TV engineering—every aspect imaginable in electronic journalism is covered. A lot of material is packed into a few months. It's an excellent course for anyone who would like to get into electronic journalism careers in radio or TV when they leave the service. The Basic Broadcasting course is open to all branches of the services. You get the benefit of graduating from an excellent journalism school and getting out of the service several years later with field experience."

★ BENEFITS TO AN OFFICER ★

For those who choose to become officers in the military and meet the qualifications, there are several

PAY GRADE	ARMY	NAVY	AIR FORCE	MARINE CORPS	COAST GUARD
O-10	GENERAL	ADMIRAL	GENERAL	GENERAL	ADMIRAL
O-9	LIEUTENANT GENERAL	VICE ADMIRAL	LIEUTENANT GENERAL	LIEUTENANT GENERAL	VICE ADMIRAL
O-8	MAJOR GENERAL	REAR ADMIRAL (UPPER HALF)	MAJOR GENERAL	MAJOR GENERAL	REAR ADMIRAL (UPPER HALF)
O-7	BRIGADIER GENERAL	REAR ADMIRAL (LOWER HALF)	BRIGADIER GENERAL	BRIGADIER GENERAL	REAR ADMIRAL (LOWER HALF)
O-6	COLONEL	CAPTAIN	COLONEL	COLONEL	CAPTAIN
O-5	LIEUTENANT COLONEL	COMMANDER	LIEUTENANT COLONEL	LIEUTENANT COLONEL	COMMANDER
O-4	MAJOR	LIEUTENANT COMMANDER	MAJOR	MAJOR	LIEUTENANT COMMANDER
O-3	CAPTAIN	LIEUTENANT	CAPTAIN	CAPTAIN	LIEUTENANT
O-2	FIRST LIEUTENANT	LIEUTENANT JUNIOR GRADE	FIRST LIEUTENANT	FIRST LIEUTENANT	LIEUTENANT JUNIOR GRADE
O-1	SECOND LIEUTENANT	ENSIGN	SECOND LIEUTENANT	SECOND LIEUTENANT	ENSIGN

Figure 2. Officer insignia of the United States armed forces

pathways that can lead to this goal, all described in detail in Chapter Five. Briefly, these are by appointment to a military academy, by enlisting in the Reserve Officers Training Program (ROTC) while in college, or by selection from the ranks of enlisted men and women for Officer Candidate School (OCS) or Officer Training School (OTS). College graduates who did not serve in ROTC programs may also be eligible for OCS or OTS.

The advantages of being an officer rather than an enlisted man or woman are chiefly in the financial rewards, prestige, and other privileges that rank can command. But there must also be a willingness and determination to accept the responsibilities that make those benefits and privileges possible. However, for officers or enlisted personnel alike, the transition from civilian to military life is never easy. Once you enlist or become a commissioned officer, you have committed yourself to serve the military and to obey all military regulations and respect all obligations for a definite period of time, as determined by your enlistment obligation.

Some find the rules, regulations, and military discipline as a whole burdensome and serve only for a short period of time before returning to civilian life. Others—like Captain Patrick J. Eberhart, an infantry officer stationed at Fort Campbell, Kentucky—adapt well and welcome the benefits of a military career and the well-financed retirement after twenty years' or more service.

★ EDUCATION IS CRUCIAL ★

"In today's Army," Captain Eberhart says, "about 98 percent of all officers have B.A. or B.S. degrees, with the approximate 2 percent who do not have degrees prevented from promotions to higher grades of rank until their degree is completed. Additionally, approximately half of all officers have master's degrees or higher. In the enlisted side of the house, college is highly encouraged, with advancement to senior noncommissioned officer ranks dependent on college education." (Captain Eberhart himself has a B.S. in accounting.)

Until he became disenchanted with his academic life-style, Patrick Eberhart had no intention of pursuing a military career. After attending Iona College in New Rochelle and then Lehman College of the City University of New York, Eberhart found the program he wanted when he enrolled in the Reserve Officers Training Program (ROTC) at Fordham University, in New York City.

"I participated in ROTC for three years with the intention of going into the Reserves," he says. "However, as my time in ROTC progressed I found I excelled in all matters related to ROTC, graduating in the top 10 percent of the class as a Distinguished Military Graduate." It was then that Eberhart "decided I liked the challenge the military life presented and decided to go on active duty. This was in 1984."

In January 1991, with more than six years of active duty behind him and having attained the rank of captain, he compared the advantages and disadvantages of military life. Chief among the advantages for him are the opportunities for responsibility, travel, and a fulfilling life-style. "As a captain I'm entrusted with the lives and welfare of 130 to 160 soldiers when I'm in a company commander role. As a brand-new lieutenant, after ROTC and nine months of training, I was entrusted with the welfare and training of a thirty-five-man platoon. This is not the standard for low-level civilian management. I also enjoy the travel. The Army has bases or positions in every continent. This provides many opportunities for meeting and enjoying different peoples and cultures."

As for life-style, "Military pay will not make you rich, but it provides you with a comfortable living. Medical benefits, housing costs, and subsistence allowances are provided. The military promotes a healthy life-style (when not at war) for physical, mental, emotional, and spiritual well-being."

Captain Eberhart has become a skilled communicator in his relations with subordinates, superiors, peers, outside agencies, "all key to selling your product from a civilian point of view." He has also honed his skills in international as well as interpersonal relations. On the international side, this includes contacts with other nations, liaison duty in other countries, and attending schools that were also attended by military personnel from other nations.

Under interpersonal relations skills he lists "how to accomplish the mission and take care of your people at the same time" and "how to make other people do what you want them to do and make them feel they want to do it." Taking an overview of military careers in general, Captain Eberhart says, "It provides great managerial/leadership training from day one and a good living for career officers and a 'good start' for noncareer officers. For many enlisted soldiers it is a great way to get out of a small or depressed city and start a new life. It broadens your horizons and your overall outlook on life."

On the advantages of military life he cites "greater maturity than my [civilian] peer group, a broader understanding of national and world politics, and much more hands-on managerial and leadership training."

He is also in a "healthy physical condition. Physical conditioning is extremely important in the military." After twenty years' service, Eberhart will be forty-two years old, he "will have 50 percent retirement pay, health care, PX/commissary privileges, and be young enough to start another career."

CHOOSING A BRANCH OF MILITARY SERVICE

T W O

Whatever branch of military service you apply to—Army, Navy, Air Force, Marine Corps, or Coast Guard—you must meet standards of good moral character, pass a physical examination, and take the Armed Services Vocational Aptitude Battery (ASVAB) test before you can be accepted. The ASVAB test will be discussed later in the chapter. What follows now is an overview of each branch of military service.

☆ THE ARMY ☆

The Army is composed of more than 85,600 officers and 536,000 enlisted men and women. The mission of the Army is to protect the security of the United States and its vital resources. It stands at the ready to defend American interests and those of its allies through land-based operations anywhere in the world. Each year the Army needs 104,000 new enlistees. To meet this demand several different periods of enlistment are offered, including two, three, four, five, and six years. Applicants must be from seventeen to thirty-five years old, high school graduates when they begin

☆ 22 ☆

The 82nd Airborne Division Marching Band, U.S. Army

active service, citizens of the United States or registered aliens, and in good health.

According to Army recruitment policies, in most cases qualified applicants can be guaranteed their choice of training or duty assignment. However, if an opening for training in a particular specialty you have selected is not available at the time of your enlistment, you can take advantage of the Army's Delayed Entry Program. This allows you to reserve a special training school or area of assignment as much as one year before you begin active duty.

Another option is the Civilian Acquired Skills Program, which recognizes skills acquired through civilian training or experience. Under this program enlistees can be promoted more quickly. The Army has the legal authority to pay a bonus of up to $12,000 as an enlistment bonus, and bonus rates are adjusted quarterly in order to attract enlistees with specialties in the areas the army needs most at a particular time. Bonuses are usually in the $1,500 to $3,500 range.

★ THE NAVY ★

The role of the Navy is to help maintain the freedom of the seas and to defend the right of the U.S. and its allies to travel and trade freely on the world's oceans. Navy sea and air power make it possible for the U.S. to use the oceans whenever and wherever our national interests happen to be. During times of war and international conflict the Navy is a vital source of U.S. defense. About 440,000 officers and enlisted men and women serve in the Navy. They operate and maintain more than 500 ships and 6,000 aircraft. Each year the Navy recruits about 80,000 officers and enlisted personnel to meet its needs.

To qualify for enlistment in Navy programs, men and women must be between the ages of seventeen

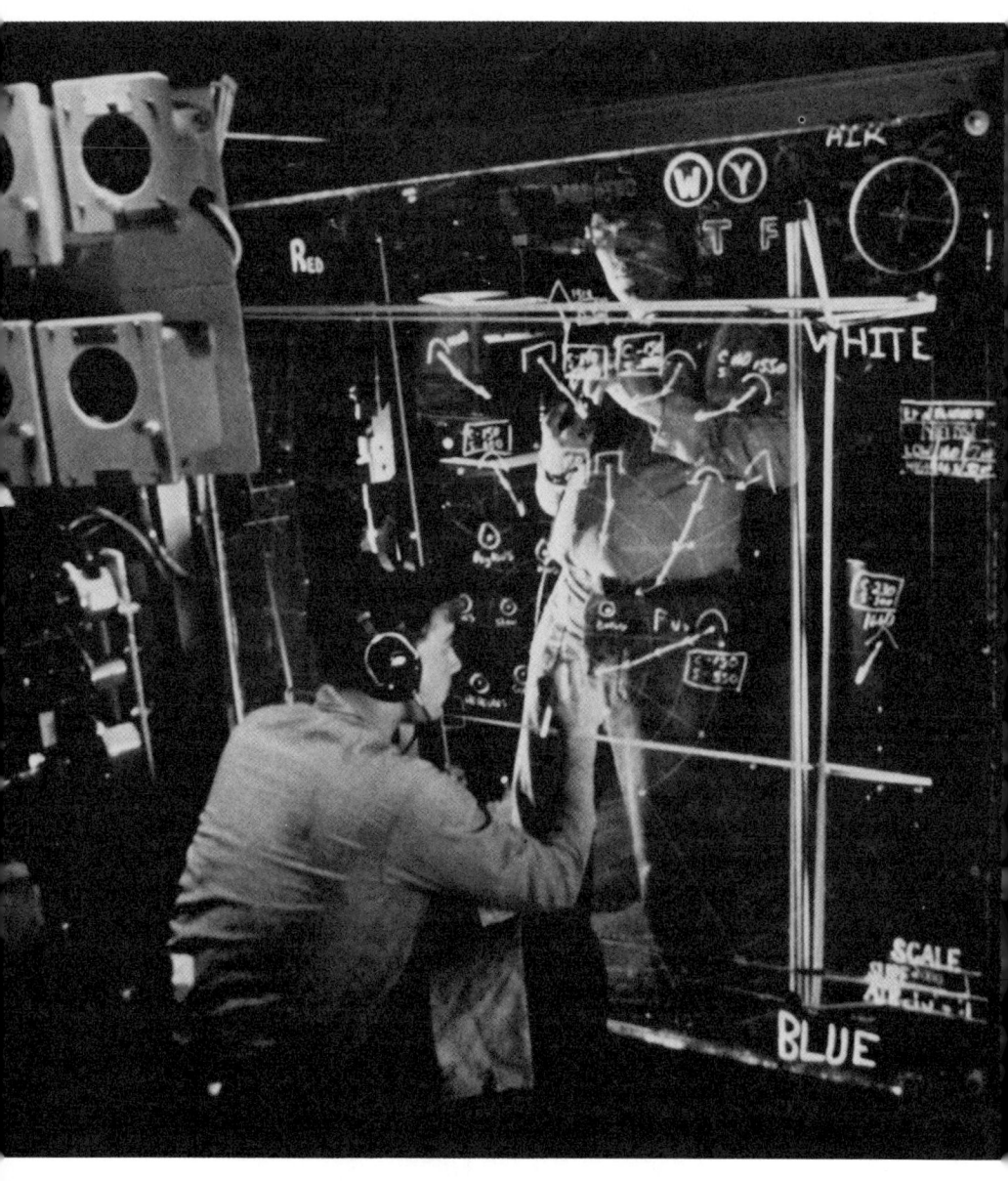

Crew members work in the combat engagement center of the battleship USS *Iowa*

and thirty-four and be high school graduates before they begin active duty. As in all branches of the military, seventeen-year-olds require parental consent to enlist. Due to extensive training requirements, those enlisting to serve in the nuclear field must not be older than twenty-three. All enlistees must be U.S. citizens or immigrant aliens with immigration and naturalization papers. The most common period of enlistment is four years; however, enlistments are available for two-, three-, five-, and six-year periods, depending on the program selected. For example, if you select a career in personnel administration you must enlist for four years. Those who select occupations in advanced electronics or the nuclear fields must enlist for six years.

After enlisting at a Military Entrance Processing Station, enlistees are usually placed in the Delayed Entry Program, which can last from a few weeks or months to up to one year, while awaiting openings for guaranteed training assignments. During this period enlistees can finish high school and take care of personal business and other pursuits while awaiting the call to active duty.

One of the enticements the Navy offers is extra pay for service aboard ships or submarines, for demolition or diving duty, for work as a crew member of an aviation team, and for certain jobs that require special training. For example, the Navy considers work in the nuclear field critical. Because of this it offers bonuses and quicker promotions when training in this field is completed and also when sailors with nuclear training reenlist.

☆ THE AIR FORCE ☆

The power and importance of the U.S. Air Force was never more apparent than in the Persian Gulf War of

Air Force technician checks the radar of an F-16 Fighting Falcon jet.

1991, which ended six weeks after it had begun with victory for the U.S. and its allies. That victory was due in large measure to the effectiveness of thousands of air strikes on Iraqi military targets. The Air Force flies and maintains a wide variety of aircraft, among them long-range bombers, supersonic fighters, and Airborne Warning and Control Systems (AWACS) aircraft. It maintains a force of 600,000 officers, airmen, and airwomen. Some of those people pilot aircraft that include everything from helicopters to the Space Shuttle. Many others do the jobs that provide vital support to the Air Force's flying mission. Each year about 60,000 men and women at least seventeen years of age are needed to fill openings.

Prior to signing on with the Air Force, enlistees who qualify, based on ASVAB and other tests, may be guaranteed to receive training in a specific skill or to be assigned within a selected aptitude area. The former is called the Guaranteed Training Enlistment Program, the latter the Aptitude Index Program. There are four aptitude areas: general, administrative, electronic, and mechanical. During basic training, skills are chosen within the selected aptitude area. The Air Force also has a Delayed Enlistment Program, under which an enlistee agrees to enter active duty on a specific date.

★ THE MARINE CORPS ★

The Marine Corps—created on November 10, 1775, by resolution of the Continental Congress in the first year of the American Revolution—takes great pride in being one of the oldest branches of the military. Marines serve on U.S. Navy ships, protect naval bases, guard U.S. embassies abroad, and serve as an ever-ready strike force to protect the U.S. and its allies anywhere in the world. The Marine Corps comprises about

U.S. Marines in combat during the Gulf War

200,000 officers and enlisted men and women with a broad range of responsibilities that go well beyond those of the typical marine foot soldiers who keep themselves in top physical condition and combat readiness. Marines also fly planes and helicopters, drive armored vehicles, gather intelligence, and survey and map territory. From 20,000 to 40,000 young men and women are needed each year to keep the Marines at full strength.

Like the other branches of military service, there is a certain amount of flexibility in periods of enlistment and in selecting a specialty. Men and women recruits can enlist for a period of three, four, five, or six years, depending on the type of enlistment program offered. Applicants must be between the ages of seventeen and twenty-nine, American citizens or registered aliens, and in good health to meet the Marines' rigorous physical training demands. As in the other branches, women can enlist in all occupation fields with the exception of combat arms—infantry, artillery, and tank and amphibian tractor crews. Women are also restricted from participating in some of the combat support and aviation operations specialties.

The Marine Corps offers a Delayed Entry Program for those who enlist but wish to finish high school or community college programs before entering active service. This allows enlistees up to one year for this purpose. One of the advantages of this program is that it allows enlistees to select training in some of the most popular but limited training programs, such as computer science and aviation specialties. There are three other enlistment options. One, called the Enlistment Option Program, guarantees qualified applicants before they enlist that they will be assigned to one of several military occupational specialties (MOS) in an MOS cluster. These clusters contain every job available in the Marine Corps, from combat arms to motor transport to high-technology avionics, electronics, and computer science. In some programs there are cash bonuses for those who qualify.

The College Enlistment Program provides incentives to all high school graduates who have post–high school degrees or vocational or community college certificates. Enlistees who qualify under this program are assigned primarily to technical occupational fields and may enlist for four, five, or six years. The third program option is called the Quality Enlistment Program and is also for assignment to primarily technical occupational fields. This program is open to high school graduates or seniors who qualify and are willing to enlist for six years. Among the incentives is the enlistee's privilege of choosing his or her assignment location.

★ THE COAST GUARD ★

In peacetime the Coast Guard is part of the Department of Transportation; but in time of war it may be placed in the Department of Defense under command of the U.S. Navy. No matter what world conditions may be at any given time, however, the Coast Guard's principal mission is to protect America's coastlines and inland waterways by enforcing customs and fishing laws, combating drug smuggling, and conducting search-and-rescue missions. It also maintains the nation's lighthouses and promotes boating safety.

This work is carried on by approximately 5,000 officers and 32,000 enlisted men and women. About 5,000 new enlistees are needed each year. To enlist in the Coast Guard you must be at least seventeen years old and younger than twenty-six on the day you enlist. Those who qualify can be guaranteed a choice of occupational training, provided openings are available. You also have the option of enlisting up to twelve months before you begin active duty.

★ THE ARMED SERVICES VOCATIONAL APTITUDE ★
BATTERY (ASVAB) TEST

All branches of the military require applicants for enlistment to take the Armed Services Vocational Aptitude Battery (ASVAB) test. This test may be taken at most high schools and is given by a test administrator from the U.S. Department of Defense. If your high school does not give the test, arrangements can be made for you to take the test at another location. The ASVAB is a three-hour test that covers ten areas of knowledge, reasoning, and skill:

1. General science
2. Arithmetic reasoning
3. Word knowledge
4. Paragraph comprehension
5. Numerical operations
6. Coding speed
7. Auto and shop information
8. Mathematics knowledge
9. Mechanical comprehension
10. Electronics information

The results of each test are scored separately and then combined to provide three academic and four occupational scores. The academic composites are measures of verbal, math, and academic ability. The occupational composites measure mechanical and crafts, business and clerical, electronics and electrical, and health, social, and technology skills.

(Right) U.S. Army engineers bore a hole for a construction project.

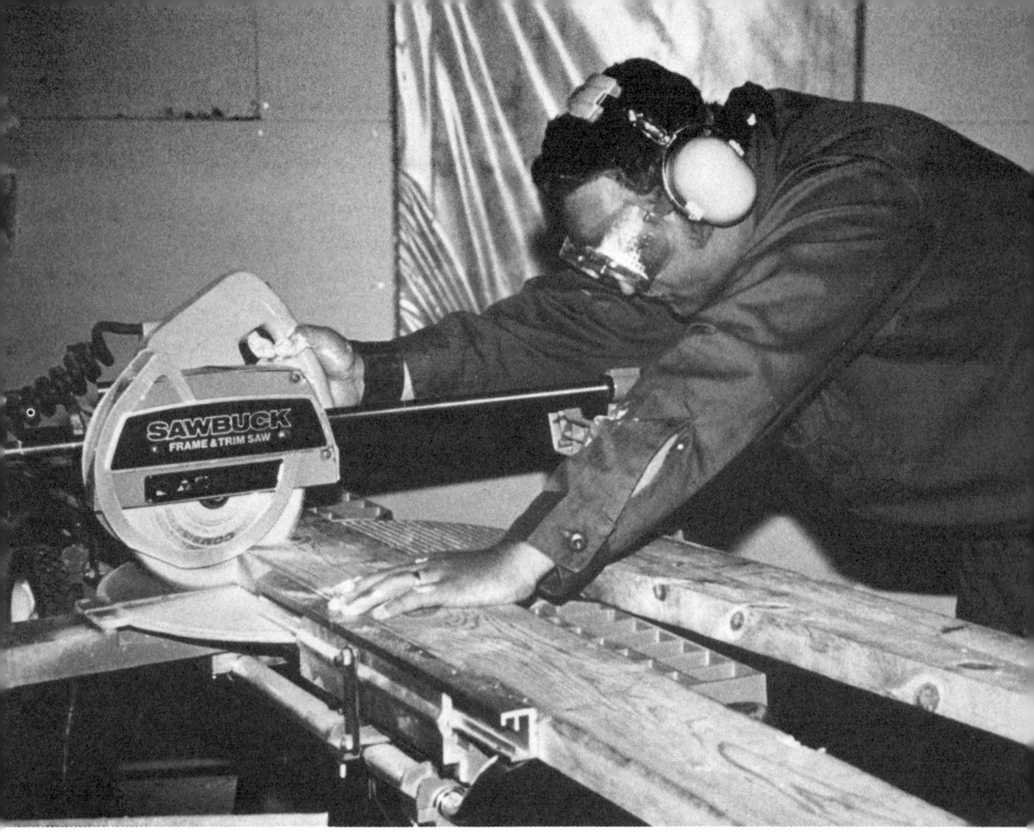
SAWBUCK
FRAME & TRIM SAW

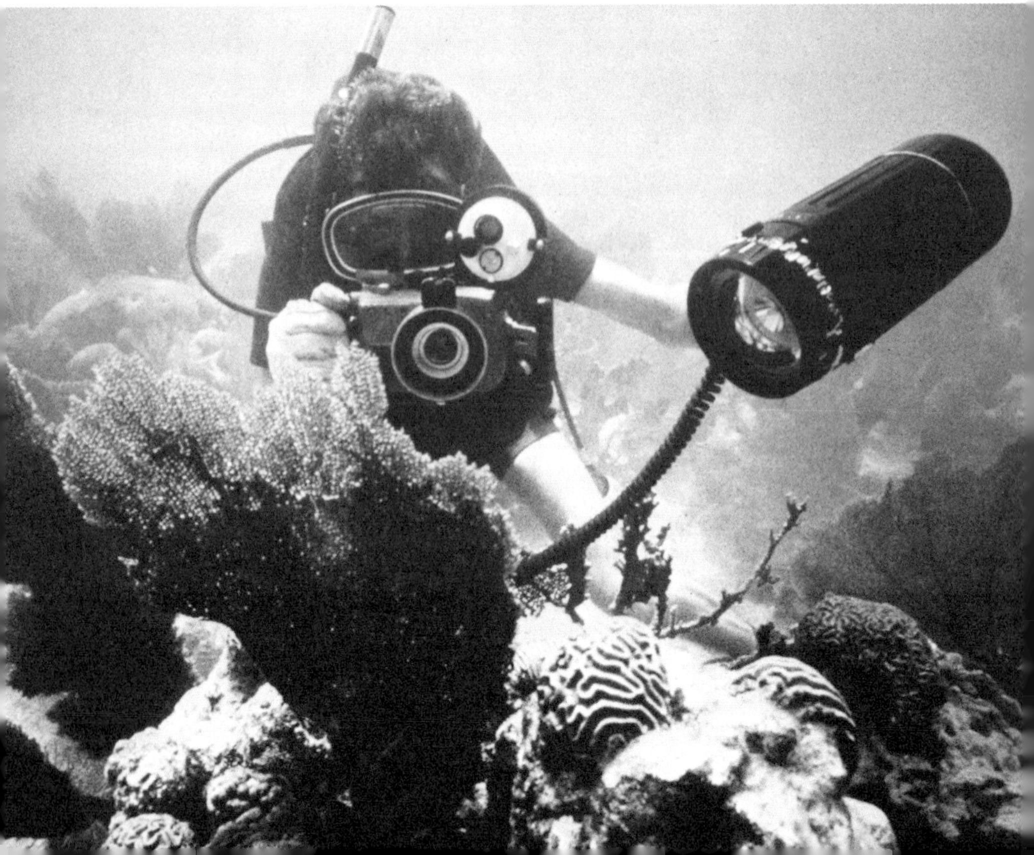

There is no charge for the ASVAB test, and no special studying is required. As in preparing for any test in school, getting a good night's rest and arriving on time are the two most important steps before the test begins. When you take the ASVAB test, you will be given a booklet containing ten short tests in the aforementioned areas. Before you take each test there are practice questions and answers to show what is expected (for examples, see Appendix A). You'll also be given a separate sheet on which to mark your answers as well as scratch paper for calculations. The person giving the test will review instructions for each test and answer any questions you may have about them before you begin.

What Test Results Indicate

Your cumulative scores in the ten tests are indications of your abilities and potential in the areas tested and in the composites that are put together from certain test scores. All of these results are measures of your aptitudes in different career areas and your potential for success in whatever career you select when you enlist in the military. The purpose of the test, as emphasized by the Department of Defense, is not to find out whether you have "passed or failed" but to find out more about your abilities and your potential for success in a particular career, if given the opportunity. To

(Facing page, top) A U.S. Navy
construction battalion unit
builder cuts wood for a window frame.

(Bottom) Member of the Navy's Fleet
Imaging Command Underwater
Photography Team (UPT) films
marine life during a training dive.

some extent your score will probably reflect how well you do in certain subjects at school. How well you score will determine the number of military career options you may qualify for.

One thing to keep uppermost in mind, whatever your ASVAB score happens to be, is that this test, like all aptitude tests, is not an absolute measurement of your abilities. Nor can it be used as an absolute predictor of how well you will do in whatever career you choose. You can feel good about test areas in which you did well, but if you did not do well in other areas, that may indicate only a lack of familiarity and experience in those particular areas.

If you have the interest and determination to learn to the best of your abilities, how well you do in your chosen career will depend on your personal efforts, training, and opportunities. Summing up, your ASVAB test score should be looked at only as an estimate of your general level of ability. The rest is up to you and the opportunities open to you to learn and progress in your chosen career.

SIGNING ON WITH UNCLE SAM

THREE

When you walk into a recruiting office, whatever branch of military service it happens to be, the first thing the person in charge will ask you to do is to fill out an application for enlistment. In some ways this is similar to a job application form. There are four parts, which request: (1) personal information; (2) school information, to be verified by your school guidance counselor; (3) information about your dependency status, for example, whether you are living with your parents or married; and (4) if you are seventeen or younger, your parent's or guardian's signature, indicating consent to your enlistment.

Once the initial interview has been completed, the next step in the recruitment process for enlisted men and women is to take the Armed Services Vocational Aptitude Battery (ASVAB) test. In order for the recruitment process to continue, you must score a minimum of 31 points. This is a percentile score. In other words, if you score 31, this means your score is higher than 30 percent of those taking the test. You and others with higher points are in the group of 70 percent who have received passing grades.

A third step in the recruiting process is to check

each applicant to find out if he or she has a police record. Any applicant who has been convicted of a felony (major crime) or more than two misdemeanors (minor crimes) will be rejected. The next step is a physical examination by a licensed doctor hired by the Department of Defense. This examination is usually performed at a Military Entrance Processing Station in a large city or major metropolitan area. Any applicant with a minor eye problem but no other major health problems will probably be accepted. However, applicants who have any problems with their hearing can expect to be rejected.

★ CHOOSING A JOB ★

Once your application has been approved and you've passed the ASVAB test and your physical examination, you are now ready for the fourth step in the recruitment process, an interview with a Job Counselor. You will be shown a list of military jobs you could qualify for, based on your ASVAB test and other test results, and asked to select the job most appealing to you. If it is available, you can then sign a contract that guarantees the job to you when you begin active duty and complete the training and educational requirements for that job. If the job you want is not available, you do not have to sign a contract. You can wait until an opening for that job becomes available. According to recruiters, the best time for high school students to enlist is before they begin their senior year. This gives them the best chance of getting the specific job specialty they want before quotas are filled. If you wait until April or May of your senior year, the number of job specialties available at that time may be much fewer.

Your choice of military career will be based on a number of factors, including your particular interests and skills as revealed by your academic record to date, your potential for achieving your career goals based on testing, and how you meet the standards set by the military for young men and women in your age group. One of the remarkable facts about the military career option is the wide spectrum of job opportunities available for enlisted men and women. For example, if your primary interest is science, the job opportunities are diverse enough to include computer-systems analysts, space-systems specialists, and environmental health specialists. If health care is the field you're most interested in, there are job opportunities for medical laboratory technicians, nursing technicians, and physical-therapy specialists. Keep in mind, however, that anyone entering the military should consider himself a soldier first, and a specialist (of any kind) second.

★ SPECIALTY: MEDICAL LABORATORY TECHNICIAN ★

In the military, just as in civilian life, medical laboratories and the technicians who operate them are an essential part of the health care system. These men and women use laboratory equipment to make tests of tissue, blood, and body fluids to detect and identify diseases in patients. They draw blood from patients, examine blood and bone marrow under microscopes, and test specimens for bacteria or viruses, recording and filing their results. They also assist in collecting specimens at autopsies (medical examinations of the dead). Military medical laboratory technicians work in medical centers, clinics, and hospitals on land or aboard ships.

There are about 6,080 medical laboratory technicians serving in the military, and about 650 new technicians are needed each year. If you choose a military career in this specialty, you will find such subjects as biology, chemistry, and algebra helpful. The ability to follow detailed procedures precisely and an

Combat specialties offer far and away the greatest number of military career opportunities. In this photo spread of training exercises, (a) marines disembark from landing craft onto beach, (b) members of the Marine detachment from the nuclear-powered aircraft carrier USS *Carl Vinson* fire M-16A1 rifles during a field exercise and (c) U.S. Navy Sea-Air-Land (SEAL) team members rappel from a UH-1 Iroquois helicopter.

b

c

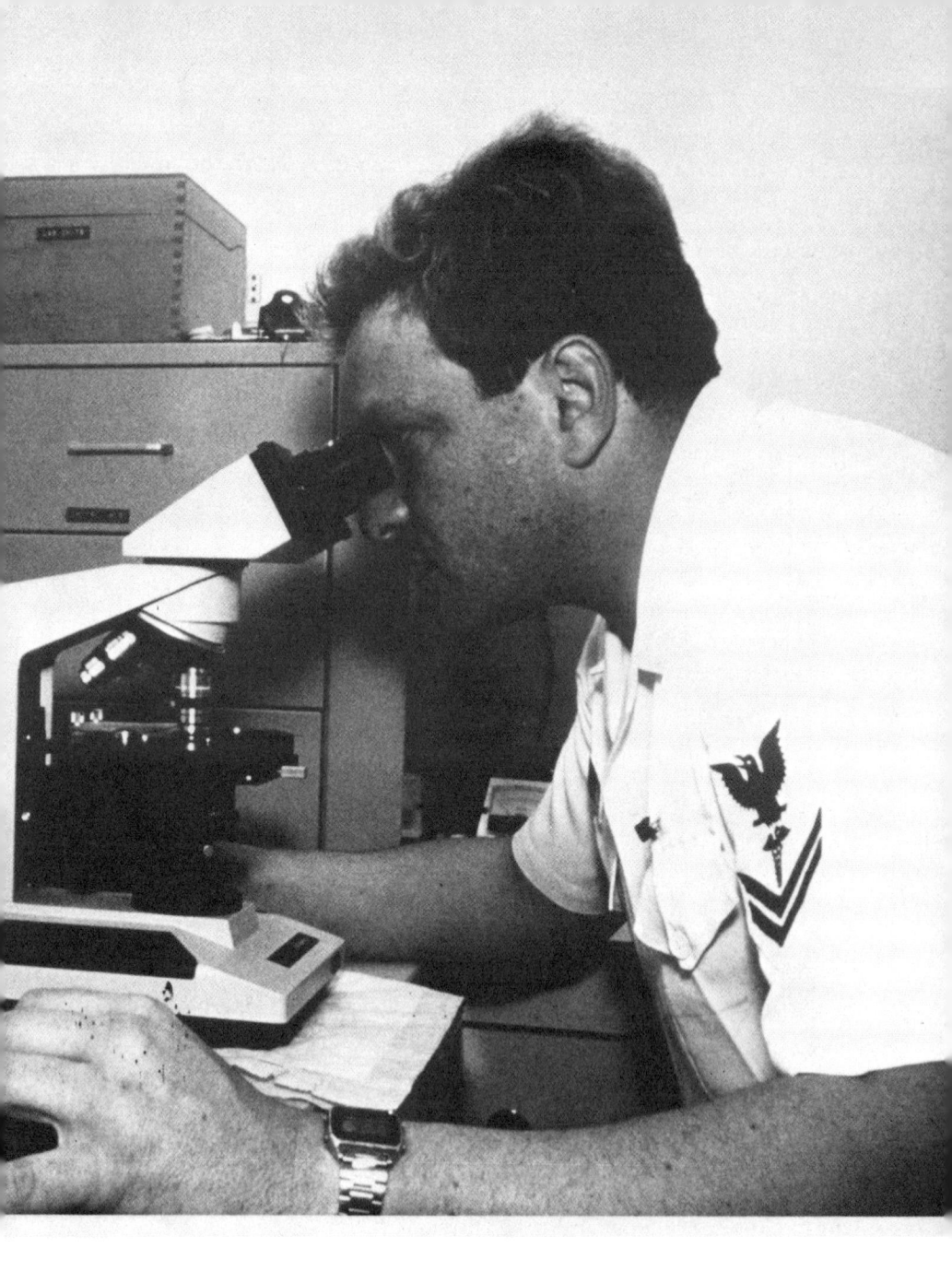

A navy medical technician uses a microscope
to take a white blood cell count.

interest in scientific and technical work are also essential.

In-service training for this specialty can last from twelve to thirty-six weeks, with classroom and on-the-job instruction that includes practice in performing tests on specimens. There are three main areas of instruction: medical laboratory procedures; studies of human parasites and diseases; and laboratory administration and record-keeping.

Trained medical laboratory technicians who return to civilian life can find similar jobs in any number of private laboratories, hospitals, clinics, and research institutions.

★ SPECIALTY: AUDIOVISUAL PRODUCTION ★

Good communication at all levels is as vital in the military as it is in civilian life. The kinds of work performed as an audiovisual production specialist mirror to a certain extent their civilian counterparts. There are military radio and television stations and films that are used for information and training. All of these activities require many different specialists to assist them, among them producers, directors, scriptwriters, and editors, as well as audiovisual production specialists. If you are selected for this specialty, you may assist producers and directors in selecting and interpreting scripts, work with writers in preparing and revising scripts, or help determine the type of presentation needed to convey the intended message.

Or you may help plan and design production scenery, graphics, and special effects, help in the planning and scheduling of audiovisual production crews, or operate media equipment and special effects devices. High school experience and/or interest in graphics, art, speech, and drama would be helpful. So would an interest in creative and artistic work, the ability to work as part of a team, and experience in school plays or making home movies.

Up to twelve weeks of classroom instruction are given as part of the training for this specialty, with courses in TV studio operations, television production, graphics, scripting, and special effects. Audiovisual production specialists are then assigned work in television, radio, or movie studios. Outdoor work would include filming or staging field exercises, sports events, or military parades and other special events.

There are about 1,600 audiovisual production specialists in the military, with a need for 170 new specialists each year. In civilian life you would find comparable jobs in advertising agencies, radio and television stations, motion picture studios, and educational and training agencies.

★ SPECIALTY: COMPUTER SYSTEMS ANALYST ★

If you are good in math, have done well in such subjects as algebra, geometry, and computer science, you might want to consider a military career as a computer systems analyst. This specialty is a natural for those who have the ability to solve abstract problems, communicate well, and have a preference for work that requires concentrated attention to detail.

One of the key jobs in the military involves the setting up of large computer systems. These systems are designed by computer systems analysts, who also design software programs that are entered into the computer where they are stored, processed, and retrieved according to the needs of the military. The quality and value of each computer system will depend on the kinds of information fed to the system, how it is processed, and, most important of all, what the system will produce. Computer systems analysts have major responsibilities in all of these areas.

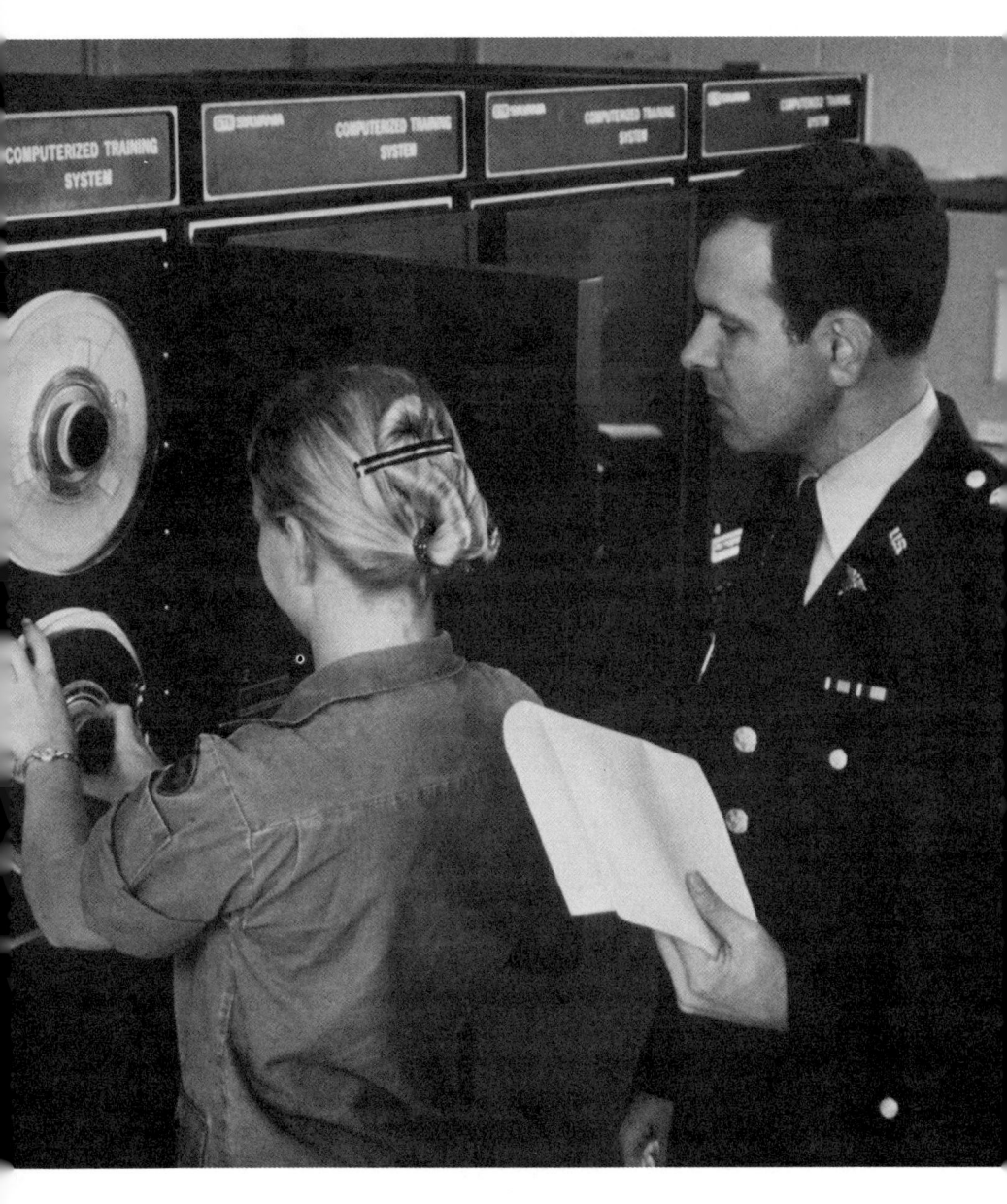

Army personnel load tapes into a computerized training system.

More specifically, it is the computer systems analyst who is responsible for some or all of the following duties:

★ Help military units determine their data processing needs
★ Develop systems plans, including input, output, and processing steps, and information storage and access methods
★ Develop flow charts, documentation, and block diagrams of systems for use by programmers
★ Help programmers program, test, and debug computer software
★ Make systems secure from unofficial access

If you apply for this specialty and are selected, you can expect job training that will include from ten to eighteen weeks of instruction in planning and designing data processing systems, methods of flow charting and documenting systems, and systems testing and evaluation. Also, there will be additional training while working in the specialty as well as advanced courses so you can broaden your responsibilities and advance in rank and pay scale. There are approximately 2,110 computer systems analysts in the military and about 220 new analysts are needed each year.

Comparable work in civilian life usually requires a four-year college degree. A wide variety of employers use programmer-analysts, systems analysts, and systems programmers. These would include banks, insurance companies, hospitals, large retailers, research firms, manufacturers, and government agencies.

★ **SPECIALTY: ENGINE MECHANIC** ★

Work as an engine mechanic is much in demand in the military to help keep a fleet of more than 50,000

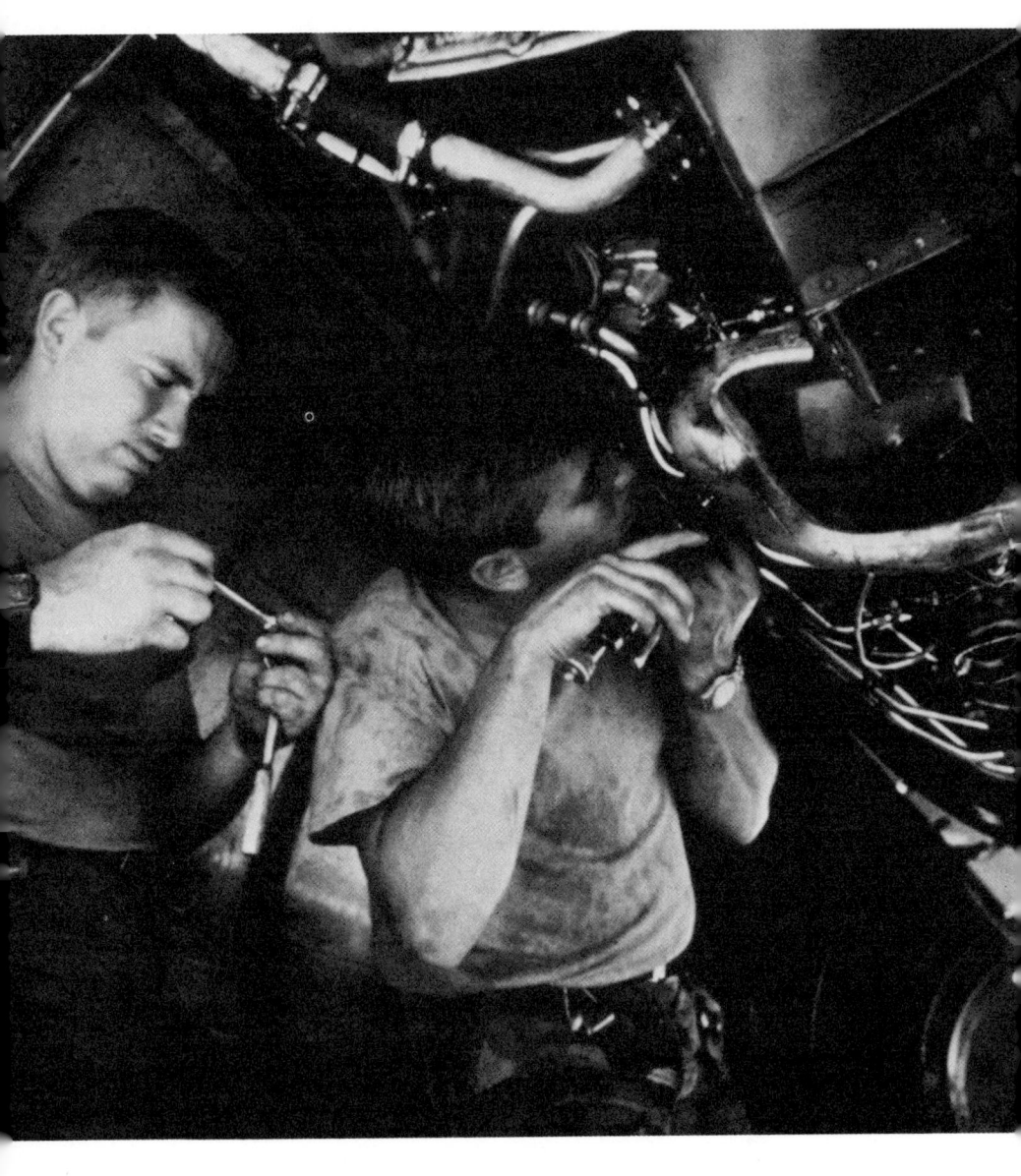

Maintenance specialists of the 320th Bomb Wing, U.S. Air Force, repair an engine on a B-52 Stratofortress aircraft.

military trucks and buses on the road. Any engine that is hard-driven needs regular maintenance, and when an engine breaks down it needs prompt repair so that the vehicle can get moving again. The engine mechanics in this specialty maintain and repair combustion engines and usually specialize by engine type, such as diesel or gasoline, or by type of vehicle, such as truck or bus. Another responsibility they have is to repair engines in mobile power generators. You will need to be in good physical condition to help lift some of the heavier engine parts, tools, and equipment.

High school subjects that will increase your chances for placement in this specialty include industrial arts and auto mechanics. It will also help if you have an interest in finding out why engines do not work and choosing the correct method of repair. You should have the ability to use hand and power tools and be able to accurately interpret charts and diagrams related to engines. There are about 20,900 engine mechanics in the military, and about 3,070 new mechanics are needed each year.

Training for this specialty consists of up to twenty-three weeks of classroom instruction and practice in repairing engines. This includes hands-on instruction in engine troubleshooting, using test equipment; disassembly and repair of gasoline and diesel engines; and maintenance and repair of fuel, electrical, and hydraulic components. Once you're assigned to a job, your training will continue. There will also be opportunities for advanced courses leading to higher pay grades. For this career specialty the Army, Navy, and Marine Corps offer Certified Apprenticeship programs.

As an engine mechanic you will be expected to perform the following duties:

★ Troubleshoot engine problems using engine analyzers and other test equipment

- ★ Adjust and repair ignition, fuel, electrical, and steering systems
- ★ Remove engines using hoists and jacks
- ★ Replace pistons, rings, and valves
- ★ Repair and replace clutches and transmissions
- ★ Lubricate engines and other vehicle parts
- ★ Keep records of repairs made and parts used

When you leave military service, experience and training in this specialty will qualify you for comparable jobs in civilian life with garages, service stations, construction firms, and truck and bus companies.

★ COMBAT SPECIALTY: INFANTRYMAN ★

If you are willing to face the dangers and threats to life and limb that combat imposes, are physically fit, and want to play a role in defending your country, you may find a career as an infantryman appealing. (Note: this specialty is not open to women.) The infantry is the military's primary land combat force. In times of peace, it will be your job as an infantryman to maintain the best possible physical condition and readiness to defend your country. In time of war it will be your job to help capture or destroy enemy ground forces and repel enemy attacks, using weapons and other equipment designed for this purpose. This means you will be putting your life on the line in defense of your country, and in protecting your own and others' lives you will be inflicting injury and death on the enemy.

The physical requirements for infantrymen are very demanding. They must perform strenuous physical activities such as marching while carrying equipment, digging foxholes, and climbing over obstacles. They must be prepared to go anywhere in the world they are needed. For this reason they work and train in all climates and weather conditions. When you are

An Army M-2 Bradley fighting
vehicle maneuvers in the desert.

taking part in training exercises that simulate real combat you will work, sleep, and eat outdoors. However, most of the time you will work on military bases.

Qualities you need to make the grade as an infantryman are a readiness to accept a challenge and face danger, the ability to stay in top physical condition, and an interest in working with others as a member of a team. All infantrymen receive basic training of seven to eight weeks, with advanced training in infantry skills that lasts another eight weeks. Some of this training takes place in the classroom, but most of the time you will spend outside in the field under simulated combat conditions. Throughout your career as an infantryman, however, your skills will be maintained through frequent squad maneuvers, target practice, and war games. War games without live ammunition allow infantrymen and other personnel to practice scouting, troop movement, surprise attack, and capturing techniques.

Your duties as an infantryman will include some or all of the following:

★ Operate, clean, and store automatic weapons, such as rifles and machine guns
★ Parachute from troop transport airplanes while carrying weapons and supplies
★ Fire armor-piercing missiles from hand-held antitank missile launchers
★ Carry out scouting missions to spot enemy troop movements and gun locations
★ Operate two-way radios and signal equipment to relay battle orders
★ Drive vehicles mounted with machine guns or small missiles
★ Perform hand-to-hand combat drills that involve martial arts tactics
★ Set firing angles and fire mortar shells at targets

★ Dig foxholes, trenches, and bunkers for protection against attacks

About 114,320 infantrymen are maintained in the military, with a need for about 22,700 new infantrymen each year. Advancement in rank and pay grade will depend on job performance and leadership ability. Although there is no equivalent to the job of infantryman in civilian life, this experience and training in teamwork, discipline, and leadership will be helpful in whatever civilian work you qualify for on release from military service.

TRAINING, BENEFITS, AND OPPORTUNITIES FOR ADVANCEMENT

FOUR

Each branch of service has its own regimen for training recruits, known as basic training, as well as career programs designed to meet its needs. However, there are many programs and benefits that all branches of service have in common. These include pay benefits and pay grades—although the rank or rating designation may differ from one branch of service to another—and opportunities for advancement. All of these advantages have increased the attractiveness of military careers for both men and women. Women especially have been opting for careers in the military in much greater numbers.

★ WOMEN IN THE MILITARY ★

In recent years the number of women in the military has grown to more than 180,000, representing about 11 percent of all active duty personnel. With the increase in the number of women has come a broadening of opportunities. Women are now eligible to apply for about 93 percent of all military career specialties, including helicopter pilot or mechanic, missile maintenance technician, satellite communications techni-

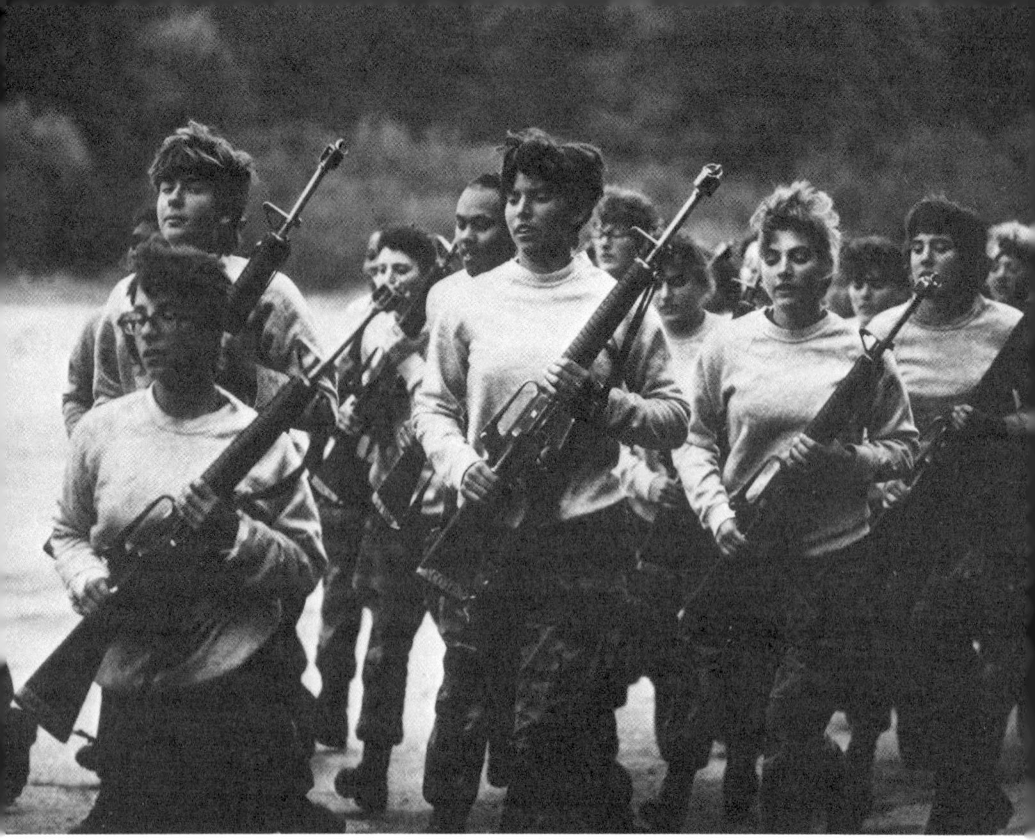

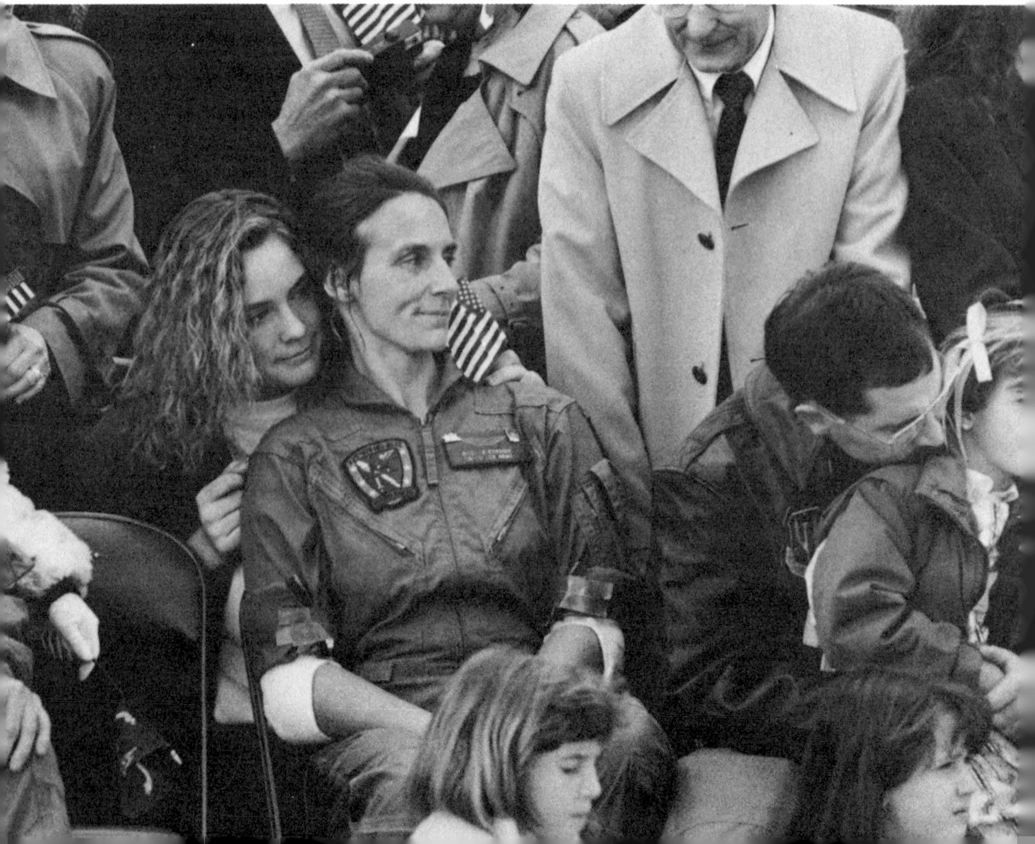

(Above) Army personnel train for close combat.

(Facing page, top) Federal laws prohibit female personnel from direct combat roles. Nevertheless, their training is rigorous.

(Bottom) Army Major Rhonda Cornum after her release as an Iraqi prisoner of war during Operation Desert Storm. She was flying a search-and-rescue mission in southern Iraq when her helicopter crashed.

cian, and heavy equipment operator. Federal laws and policies have prevented women from being assigned duty that involves a high exposure to direct combat. For this reason women are not eligible for such occupations as tank crew member, fighter pilot, submarine crew member, or infantryman. There has been an increasing opposition to this restriction from some advocates of women's rights. However the controversy is resolved, the fact remains that women have a wide choice of career opportunities, share the same pay scales for their rank, and have the same opportunities for advancement as their male counterparts.

★ PAY AND BENEFITS ★

Military personnel in all five services are paid according to the same pay scale and receive the same benefits as set by the U.S. Congress (see Tables 1 and 2). The annual pay per grade or rating is usually bolstered each year by a cost-of-living increase. For enlisted personnel, the military also provides basic necessities in addition to pay. These include food, clothing, housing, and full medical care. Enlisted personnel can advance through nine pay grades, with pay determined by grade or ranking and length of service. In other words, the higher your rating and the longer you remain in the military, the higher your pay will be. Illustrations on the following pages show pay grades and insignia for each of the five branches of the military as well as basic pay and a summary of benefits.

Except for recruits who have certain technical skills that entitle them to begin at a higher pay grade, recruits begin at pay grade E-1 and within six months usually advance to E-2. The next promotion, to grade E-3, will come within the next six to twelve months if your job performance is satisfactory and you meet other requirements. Thereafter, promotions to the rank of E-4 and higher are based on several factors: job performance, leadership ability, promotion test scores, years or service, and time in present pay grade. At the higher pay grades promotions are more competitive.

★ THE GI BILL ★

Unless you choose not to participate, as soon as you begin active duty you will be enrolled in the Veterans Educational Assistance Benefit Program, known as the GI Bill. This means your basic pay will be reduced by $100 per month for your first twelve months of service. However, once you have completed three years of continuous active duty you will be eligible for $300 per month for thirty-six months up to a maximum of $10,000 in basic benefits for full-time schooling. Those who fulfill a two-year service obligation are entitled to $250 per month for thirty-six months.

★ FINANCIAL INCENTIVES ★

Financial incentives for enlisted personnel who qualify include extra pay for certain types of duty, such as submarine and flight duty. Similar incentives are given to those involved in such hazardous or special assignments as parachute jumping, flight-deck duty, explosives demolition, sea duty, diving duty, and duty in certain foreign countries and in areas subject to hostile fire. As an added incentive, bonuses are paid to those who select certain occupations.

The Army's Student Loan "Forgiveness"

The army has a special incentive to offer enlistees who have attended college and have outstanding student loans. For each year of Army service, the Army will

Table 1. Monthly Pay for Military Personnel in 1992 (includes 4.2%

Grade	Less than 2	2	3	4	6	8	10	12	14

Commissioned officers

Grade	Less than 2	2	3	4	6	8	10	12	14
O-10	6417.60	6643.50	6643.50	6643.50	6643.50	6898.20	6898.20	7280.40	7280.40
O-9	5687.70	5836.50	5961.00	5961.00	5961.00	6112.50	6112.50	6366.90	6366.90
O-8	5151.60	5306.10	5431.80	5431.80	5431.80	5836.50	5836.50	6112.50	6112.50
O-7	4280.40	4571.40	4571.40	4571.40	4776.60	4776.60	5053.50	5053.50	5306.10
O-6	3172.80	3485.70	3714.30	3714.30	3714.30	3714.30	3714.30	3714.30	3840.30
O-5	2537.40	2979.30	3185.40	3185.40	3185.40	3185.40	3281.70	3458.40	3690.30
O-4	2138.70	2604.60	2778.30	2778.30	2829.90	2954.70	3156.30	3333.60	3485.70
O-3	1987.50	2222.40	2375.70	2628.60	2754.30	2853.00	3007.50	3156.30	3233.70
O-2	1733.10	1892.70	2274.30	2350.50	2399.40	2399.40	2399.40	2399.40	2399.40
O-1	1504.80	1566.30	1892.70	1892.70	1892.70	1892.70	1892.70	1892.70	1892.70

Officers with more than 4 years active duty as enlisted or warrant officer

Grade	Less than 2	2	3	4	6	8	10	12	14
O-3E	0.00	0.00	0.00	2628.60	2754.30	2853.00	3007.50	3156.30	3281.70
O-2E	0.00	0.00	0.00	2350.50	2399.40	2475.60	2604.60	2704.60	2778.30
O-1E	0.00	0.00	0.00	1892.70	2022.30	2096.70	2172.60	2248.20	2350.50

Warrant officers

Grade	Less than 2	2	3	4	6	8	10	12	14
W-5	0.00	0.00	0.00	0.00	0.00	0.00	0.00	0.00	0.00
W-4	2025.00	2172.60	2172.60	2222.40	2323.20	2425.80	2527.50	2704.20	2829.90
W-3	1840.50	1996.50	1996.50	2022.30	2045.70	2195.40	2323.20	2399.40	2475.60
W-2	1611.90	1743.90	1743.90	1794.90	1892.70	1996.50	2072.10	2148.30	2222.40
W-1	1342.80	1539.90	1539.90	1668.30	1743.90	1818.90	1892.70	1971.00	2045.70

Enlisted members

Grade	Less than 2	2	3	4	6	8	10	12	14
E-9	0.00	0.00	0.00	0.00	0.00	0.00	2355.90	2408.70	2463.30
E-8	0.00	0.00	0.00	0.00	0.00	1975.50	2031.90	2085.60	2139.60
E-7	1379.10	1488.90	1544.10	1598.10	1652.40	1705.20	1759.80	1814.70	1896.90
E-6	1186.80	1293.30	1347.30	1404.60	1457.10	1509.60	1565.10	1645.80	1697.40
E-5	1041.30	1133.40	1188.60	1240.20	1321.80	1375.50	1430.10	1482.60	1509.60
E-4	971.10	1025.70	1086.00	1170.00	1216.20	1216.20	1216.20	1216.20	1216.20
E-3	915.00	965.40	1003.80	1043.40	1043.40	1043.40	1043.40	1043.40	1043.40
E-2	880.50	880.50	880.50	880.50	880.50	880.50	880.50	880.50	880.50
E-1	785.70	785.70	785.70	785.70	785.70	785.70	785.70	785.70	785.70

E-1 with less than 4 months—$726.60

Note: Basic pay is limited to $8,733.30 per month by level V of the executive pay schedule.

Source: The *Army Times*

pay hike from previous year)

16	18	20	22	26
7801.20	7801.20	8323.50	8323.50	8733.30
6898.20	6898.20	7280.40	7280.40	7801.20
6366.90	6643.50	6898.20	7068.30	7068.30
5836.50	6238.20	6238.20	6238.20	6238.20
4447.50	4674.60	4776.60	5053.50	5480.70
3966.60	4193.70	4320.90	4471.80	4471.80
3638.70	3739.20	3739.20	3739.20	3739.20
3233.70	3233.70	3233.70	3233.70	3233.70
2399.40	2399.40	2399.40	2399.40	2399.40
1892.70	1892.70	1892.70	1892.70	1892.70
3281.70	3281.70	3281.70	3281.70	3281.70
2778.30	2778.30	2778.30	2778.30	2778.30
2350.50	2350.50	2350.50	2350.50	2350.50
0.00	0.00	3455.90	3587.10	3846.30
2929.20	3007.50	3104.70	3208.50	3458.40
2549.40	2628.60	2730.90	2829.90	2929.20
2300.40	2375.70	2450.70	2549.40	2549.40
2121.90	2195.40	2274.30	2274.30	2274.30
2519.70	2576.10	2626.20	2763.90	3032.70
2196.30	2246.70	2301.90	2436.90	2708.40
1950.60	2004.90	2031.00	2167.20	2436.90
1752.30	1779.00	1779.00	1779.00	1779.00
1509.60	1509.60	1509.60	1509.60	1509.60
1216.20	1216.20	1216.20	1216.20	1216.20
1043.40	1043.40	1043.40	1043.40	1043.40
880.50	880.50	880.50	880.50	880.50
785.70	785.70	785.70	785.70	785.70

ATPCO

Basic Allowance for Quarters

Grade	Without Full	Without Partial	With Dependents
O-10	689.40	50.70	848.10
O-9	689.40	50.70	848.10
O-8	689.40	50.70	848.10
O-7	689.40	50.70	848.10
O-6	632.40	39.60	764.10
O-5	609.00	33.00	736.20
O-4	564.30	26.70	649.20
O-3	452.40	22.20	537.30
O-2	358.80	17.70	458.70
O-1	302.10	13.20	409.80
O-3E	488.40	22.20	577.20
O-2E	415.20	17.70	520.80
O1-E	357.00	13.20	481.20
W-5	573.00	25.20	626.40
W-4	509.10	25.20	574.20
W-3	427.80	20.70	526.50
W-2	379.80	15.90	484.20
W-1	318.30	13.80	418.80
E-9	418.20	18.60	551.10
E-8	384.30	15.30	507.90
E-7	327.90	12.00	471.90
E-6	296.70	9.90	436.20
E-5	273.60	8.70	392.10
E-4	238.20	8.10	341.10
E-3	233.70	7.80	317.40
E-2	190.20	7.20	302.10
E-1	168.90	6.90	302.10

Basic Allowance for Subsistence

Officers $134.42 a month
(including commissioned officers, warrants and aviation cadets)

Enlisted	<4 mos.	Others
Rations in kind not available	$6.68	$7.23
On leave or granted permission to mess separately	$5.92	$6.41
Emergency conditions where no government messing is available	$8.86	$9.59

Table 2. Summary of Employment Benefits for Enlisted Members

Vacation	Leave time of 30 days per year.
Medical, Dental, and Eye Care	Full medical, hospitalization, dental, and eye care services for enlistees and most health care costs for family members.
Continuing Education	Voluntary educational programs for undergraduate and graduate degrees or for single courses, including tuition assistance for programs at colleges and universities.
Recreational Programs	Programs include athletics, entertainment, and hobbies: Softball, basketball, football, swimming, tennis, golf, weight training, and other sports Parties, dances, and entertainment Club facilities, snack bars, game rooms, movie theaters, and lounges Active hobby and craft clubs, book and music libraries.
Exchange and Commissary Privileges	Food, goods, and services are available at military stores, generally at lower costs.
Legal Assistance	Many free legal services are available to assist with personal matters.

Source: Department of Defense

"forgive" one third of the loan up to a maximum of $55,000. Thus, in three years the loan will be repaid in full.

★ ALLOWANCES FOR OFF-BASE LIVING ★

In your first year of service you will be living in military housing and eating in military dining facilities free of charge. However, when you live off-base you will receive allowances for housing and for food in addition to your basic pay. In 1992 the monthly housing allowance ranged from $162 to $528.90, depending on pay grade and number of dependents (for example, if you are married). Food allowances range from $170.40 to $276.00 per month, depending on your living circumstances. Allowances are not considered taxable income and for this reason represent a tax saving in addition to their cash value.

Other benefits include medical, dental, and eye care, vacation or leave time of thirty days per year, legal assistance in handling personal matters, and food, goods, and services at military stores at much lower cost than you would pay off-base. There are also many educational benefits, and these will be discussed within each branch of service.

If you retire after twenty years of active duty you will receive monthly payments for the rest of your life equivalent to 40 percent of the average basic pay for your last five years of active duty. After thirty years of active service, you can retire and receive 75 percent of basic pay. Other retirement benefits include medical care and the privilege to purchase food, goods, and services on military bases. You will also be eligible for veterans benefits such as guarantees for home loans, hospitalization, survivor benefits, and assistance in finding civilian employment so you can continue your career in civilian life.

★ ARMY TRAINING ★

Basic training in the Army consists of eight weeks of rigorous orientation for men and women recruits. During this intensive period, you will be expected to acquire the discipline, spirit, pride, knowledge, and physical conditioning necessary to perform your duties according to Army standards. There are Army training centers in New Jersey, South Carolina, Georgia, Texas, Kentucky, Alabama, Oklahoma, and Missouri.

Teamwork is stressed. Recruits are trained in groups called platoons, ranging in size from nine to about eighty soldiers. The schedule is intentionally demanding in order to inculcate the importance of discipline in order to succeed in military life. Classes are given along with field instruction. These include training in military life, weapons firing, physical conditioning, and military drill. Classes in human relations show how men and women from different backgrounds can learn how to work closely together as a team. Personal time or off-duty time is much more limited during basic training than it will be once training is completed.

After basic training, those who have selected a career specialty will be sent to an Advanced Individual Training (AIT) school. These schools are located at Army bases throughout the country. AIT students attend traditional classes, similar to a high school or college setting. Depending on the specialty, there will be demonstrations by qualified instructors and practical exercises to allow trainees to use the tools, equipment, and procedures required by their specialty. In many cases there will be on-the-job training where skills are learned while working with qualified specialists. Many AIT courses are registered with the U.S. Department of Labor as Certified Apprenticeship Training Programs, which helps to guarantee civilian employment in that particular specialty.

★ PROGRESSIVE SERVICE SCHOOL TRAINING ★

The Army promotes participation in its Progressive Service School Training Program as a means for men and women to advance in their careers. Some schooling is on a voluntary basis, but in other cases soldiers are selected on a competitive basis. As soldiers progress to higher levels they become eligible for advanced technical training. Two examples of this are the advanced noncommissioned officers courses at the E-6 grade level and the Sergeants Major Academy at the E-8 and E-9 grade levels.

Education off-base or at the civilian level is also encouraged as a means of improving work performance and preparedness for life in a technical and competitive society. Under the aegis of the Army Continuing Education System, counseling and academic and vocational-technical services are provided either at no charge or at minimal cost. Limited tuition assistance is given to those who wish to take college courses on their own time.

★ NAVY TRAINING ★

The Navy describes basic training as "a tough eight-week period of transition from civilian to Navy life. It provides the discipline, knowledge, and physical conditioning necessary to continue serving in the Navy." The Navy has three basic-training centers: Orlando, Florida; Great Lakes, Illinois; and San Diego, California. However, women recruits train only at Orlando. The day starts at 0530 (5:30 a.m.) and ends with taps (lights out) at 2130 (9:30 p.m.). The daily schedule during weekdays (Monday through Friday) includes eleven periods of physical fitness and classroom instruction, each lasting forty minutes.

Physical fitness training includes push-ups, sit-ups, jumping jacks, distance running, water survival, and instruction in swimming. All recruits are tested for their physical fitness at the beginning and at the end of basic training. More than thirty subjects are covered in the classroom and field instruction. These include aircraft and ship familiarization, basic deck seamanship, career incentives, decision-making, time management, military drill, Navy mission and organization, military customs and courtesies, and the chain of command.

Job Training and Promotions

Once recruit training is completed, most sailors go directly to the technical school, called a Class A school, that they signed up for when they enlisted. Class A schools are located at Navy bases throughout the U.S. Among the chief education centers, in addition to Great Lakes and San Diego, are Navy bases in Newport, Rhode Island, and Pensacola, Florida. Technical schooling can run from a few weeks to many months, depending on the specialty. Those who complete recruit training but are undecided about a career specialty can begin an on-the-job apprenticeship program. One such program for men is the Subfarer Program, which trains them for service aboard submarines. One of the pluses in Navy schooling is that the Office of Education Credit of the American Council on Education regularly reviews and evaluates Navy training. Nearly all Navy courses have been recommended by the Council for college and university credit.

Navy Campus

The Navy has a program called Navy Campus that allows enlisted men and women to take educational courses throughout their Navy careers. All levels of education and training can be pursued, from high school equivalency to vocational certificates to college degrees. This program includes both on-duty and off-duty study.

Promotion to higher ratings in the Navy is similar to that in the other services. It is based on five considerations: job performance, competitive examination grades, recommendations of supervisors, length of service, and time in present level of work. However, Navy men and women with highly developed skills in certain areas, such as electronics and the nuclear field, may advance more rapidly.

☆ **AIR FORCE TRAINING** ☆

All basic training in the Air Force is conducted at Lackland Air Force Base (AFB) in San Antonio, Texas. It lasts six weeks, two weeks less than basic training in the Army or Navy. There are four main areas of training: academic instruction; courses to build confidence; physical conditioning; and marksmanship. If you enlist in the Air Force without indicating preference for a particular career specialty, you will receive individual counseling to help choose a job in line with Air Force needs and your own aptitudes and desires.

The Air Force maintains training centers for formal, in-residence training at Chanute AFB, Rantoul, Illinois; Keesler AFB, Biloxi, Mississippi; Lowry AFB, Denver, Colorado; as well as at three bases in Texas: Lackland in San Antonio, Sheppard in Wichita Falls, and Goodfellow in San Angelo. At these and other locations in the U.S., airmen receive instruction and hands-on training in their specialties.

After basic training, some airmen go directly to their first duty station and begin receiving on-the-job training, depending on the specialty selected. Whether trained formally or on the job, however, airmen continue their education and training in a two-part program that consists of self-study and supervised job performance.

Community College of the Air Force

Unique among the services, the Community College of the Air Force (CCAF) offers educational programs directly related to Air Force specialties. Those who graduate from CCAF receive an associate in applied science degree. CCAF works with Air Force training schools, regional accrediting agencies, and hundreds of cooperating colleges and universities. Through CCAF airmen and airwomen can earn fully recognized college credits for most of what they learn through courses and on-the-job training. There are courses in more than eighty fields of study, ranging from police science to environmental services technology.

Two other educational opportunities are the College Level Examination Program, which makes it possible for airmen and airwomen to receive credit for selected college courses by examination, and the Extension Course Institute (ECI). ECI is the Air Force's correspondence school, offering free of charge nearly 400 courses, "everything from fundamentals of solid state devices to apprentice carpentry." There are also courses in auto mechanics, plumbing, and electrical wiring for background knowledge. For most college-level courses the Air Force will pay for 75 to 90 percent of the tuition costs.

★ MARINE CORPS TRAINING ★

Marine Corps basic training for women recruits is conducted at Parris Island, South Carolina. Men recruits train either at Parris Island or in San Diego, California. In the Marine Corps tradition, basic training in this branch of the military is "rigorous, demanding, and challenging." All recruits are assigned to a platoon, receive an additional physical examination, and take further assignment classification tests. Each platoon is led by a team of three drill instructors. A recruit's day begins with reveille at 0500 (5:00 a.m.) and continues with drill, physical training, and classes in weapons and conduct, ending with taps at 2100 (9:00 p.m.).

When basic training is completed, each recruit is given a short period of leave before beginning formal school training or on-the-job instruction in his or her chosen career specialty. In the Marine Corps there are more than 200 basic formal schools and 300 advanced schools. Instruction and training may last from a few weeks to more than a year. This will depend on the level of technical expertise and knowledge expected for a marine to become proficient in a particular job skill.

A Marine officer candidate in training in Quantico, Virginia

Certain military occupation specialties (MOS's) in the electric and electronics fields may require from ten to fifty weeks of training, while training for a machinery mechanic may range from six to eighteen weeks. As soon as possible, trainees are placed in actual work environments to obtain practical experience and develop confidence. Performance requirements in many Marine MOS's are comparable to those for certified or licensed skilled workers in civilian occupations. With this in mind, many marines apply for status as a registered apprentice in such specialties as air traffic control, electricity, and surveying.

The Meritorious Promotion System

Job advancement or promotion in the Marines is similar to other branches of military service. However, those who qualify under the Meritorious Promotion System are recognized for outstanding job performance and competence and advance more quickly. All candidates for accelerated advancement are carefully screened by a commanding officer's promotion board.

The Marine Corps believes strongly that "a better educated marine is a better marine." All marines are encouraged to continue their education by taking advantage of service schools and Marine Corps funded off-duty courses at local colleges and universities. One program, the Marine Corps Basic Skills Education Program, provides fully funded instruction in English, English as a second language, reading, and mathematics for anyone who is found to be deficient in one or more of these skills.

Opportunity Colleges

Another program promoted by the Marine Corps is the Servicemembers Opportunity Colleges (SOC) system, which includes a consortium of more than 400 colleges and universities throughout the U.S. These educational institutions have agreed to help military personnel gain access to higher education by minimizing residency requirements and recognizing such nontraditional endeavors as the College Level Examination Program. This program makes it easier to transfer college credits and also grants credit for formal military training.

★ COAST GUARD TRAINING ★

In the Coast Guard as well as in the Navy, basic training is known as "boot camp." This lasts about eight weeks in the Coast Guard and is held at Cape May, New Jersey. Instruction is given in Coast Guard history, missions, customs, and basic disciplines as well as physical training and application of the subjects studied. After basic training, Coast Guard men and women are sent to Petty Officer Class A schools for training in occupational specialties. These programs range from ten to forty-two weeks of study, depending on the rating or specialty. Study and training in these schools leads to advancement to petty officer third class. There are other opportunities for education and training for those who qualify at Advanced Petty Officer and Special schools.

Tuition Assistance Program

Off-duty education is encouraged through the Tuition Assistance Program. This program permits both enlistees and officers to enroll at accredited colleges, universities, and other schools. The Coast Guard pays the tuition for all courses not in excess of six credits per semester or quarter, and also for any courses not extending beyond one semester or seventeen weeks, whichever is longer.

Physician's Assistant Program

A special program promoted by the Coast Guard for those who qualify is the Physician's Assistant Program. This is a two-year, full-time course of study at Duke University Medical Center, Durham, North Carolina. The program comprises nine months' study of elementary scientific principles, terminology, and basic medical science, plus fifteen months of clinical training. Graduates receive certificates as physician's assistants and a commission as chief warrant officer. In cases where a student has had other college courses, completion of the program may earn him or her a bachelor's degree in health science.

Advanced Electronics Training

Another program unique to the Coast Guard is the Advanced Electronics Training Program for enlisted personnel. This program is conducted at several locations throughout the country. The courses given provide a practical mix of theory and current state-of-the-art electronics leading to duty as an engineer's assistant. Engineer's assistants participate in the design and specification of equipment and equipment modification at headquarters units, at district offices, on major vessels, and at larger shore units.

MAKING THE GRADE AS AN OFFICER

FIVE

If you would like to serve as an officer in one of the branches of the military, you will find the same broad range of career opportunities available to enlisted men and women, but with a distinct difference. As an officer your pay and other benefits will be much higher and your responsibilities much greater. So are the educational requirements, which include a minimum of a bachelor's degree, the culmination of four years of college (see Table 3). Officers in the military are comparable to executives and professionals in civilian life. Many military officer specialties are almost exact parallels.

For example, military doctors, dentists, nurses, and therapists provide health care to military personnel and their families. Military lawyers provide the legal expertise and work in handling legal matters. There are military scientists, engineers, and other technologists who perform responsibilities similar to their civilian counterparts, but in a military setting. All military airplane and helicopter pilots are officers. Officers are the leaders in all phases of combat operations, such as special operations, the infantry, armor, missiles, artillery, and naval operations. All in all, there

Table 3. General Officer Qualifications*

Age	Must be between 19 and 29 years for OCS/OTS; 17 and 21 years for ROTC; 17 and 22 years for the service academies.
Citizenship Status	Must be U.S. citizen.
Physical Condition	Must meet minimum physical standards listed below. Some occupations have additional physical standards. Height— For males: Maximum—6'8" Minimum—5'0" For females: Maximum—6'8" Minimum—4'10" Weight—There are minimum and maximum weights, according to age and height, for males and females. Vision—There are minimum vision standards. Overall Health—Must be in good health and pass a medical exam. Certain diseases or conditions may exclude persons from enlistment, such as diabetes, severe allergies, epilepsy, alcoholism, and drug addiction.
Education	Must have a four-year college degree from an accredited institution. Some occupations require advanced degrees or four-year degrees in a particular field.
Aptitude	Must achieve the minimum entry score on an officer qualification test. Each service uses its own officer qualification test.
Moral Character	Must meet standards designed to screen out persons unlikely to become successful officers. Standards cover court convictions, juvenile delinquency, arrests, and drug use.
Marital Status and Dependents	May be either single or married for ROTC, OCS/OTS, and direct appointment pathways. Must be single to enter and graduate from service academies. Single persons with one or more minor dependents are not eligible for officer commissioning.
Waivers	On a case-by-case basis, exceptions (waivers) are granted by individual services for some of the above qualification requirements. *Each service sets its own qualification requirements for officers.

Source: Department of Defense

are more than 1,500 officer job specialties. They fall into the following nine broad groupings:

1. Combat specialties
2. Executive, administrative, and management
3. Human services
4. Media and public affairs
5. Health diagnosing and testing
6. Health care
7. Engineering, science, and other technology
8. Service occupations
9. Transportation

The demand is high for those who would make good officers in the Army, Navy, Air Force, Marine Corps, and Coast Guard. Each year about 20,000 men and women become commissioned officers. If you would like to join the military as an officer, without any previous military experience, you must have a four-year college degree. However, if you want to be an officer in certain scientific, technical, or professional fields, an advanced degree is required. Whatever the branch of service, you must meet high standards of mental aptitude, be physically fit, and have a good moral character. There are four ways in which you can become an officer: (1) by attending and graduating from military academies; (2) by completing a Reserve Officers Training Corps (ROTC) program while attending college; (3) by graduating from Officer Candidate or Officer Training School (OCS or OTS); and (4) by direct appointment.

✯ APPLYING TO MILITARY ACADEMIES ✯

There are four military academies: the United States Military Academy at West Point, New York, for the Army; the United States Naval Academy, Annapolis,

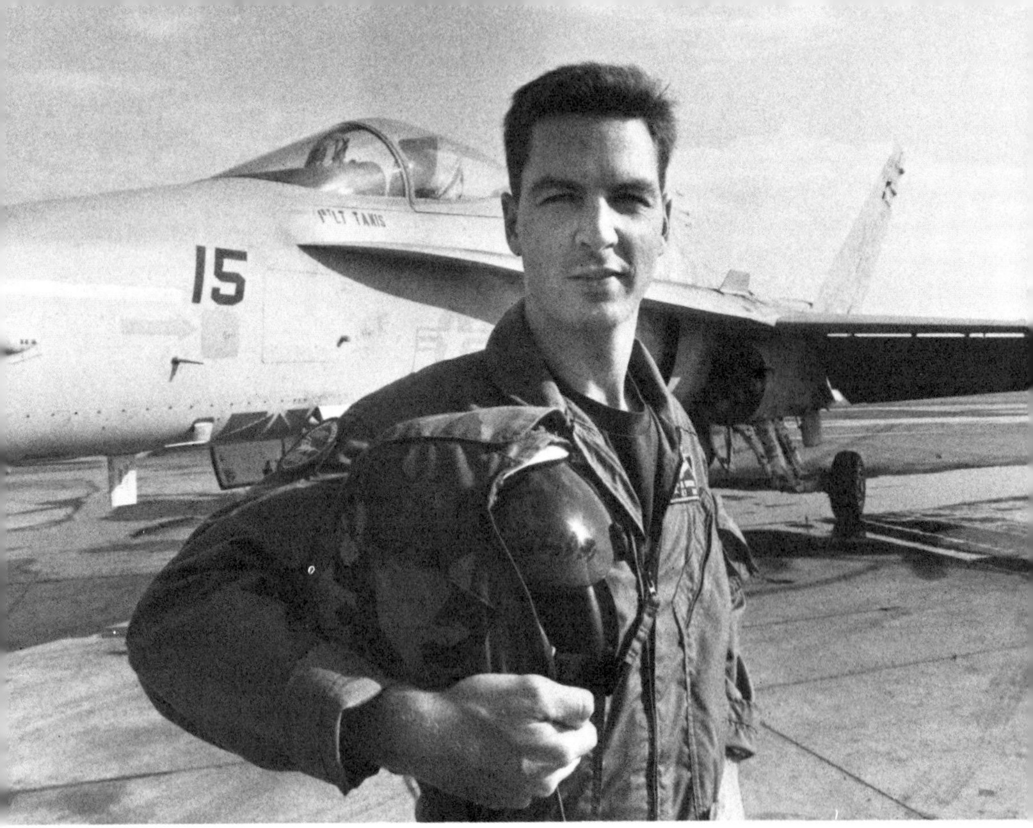
15

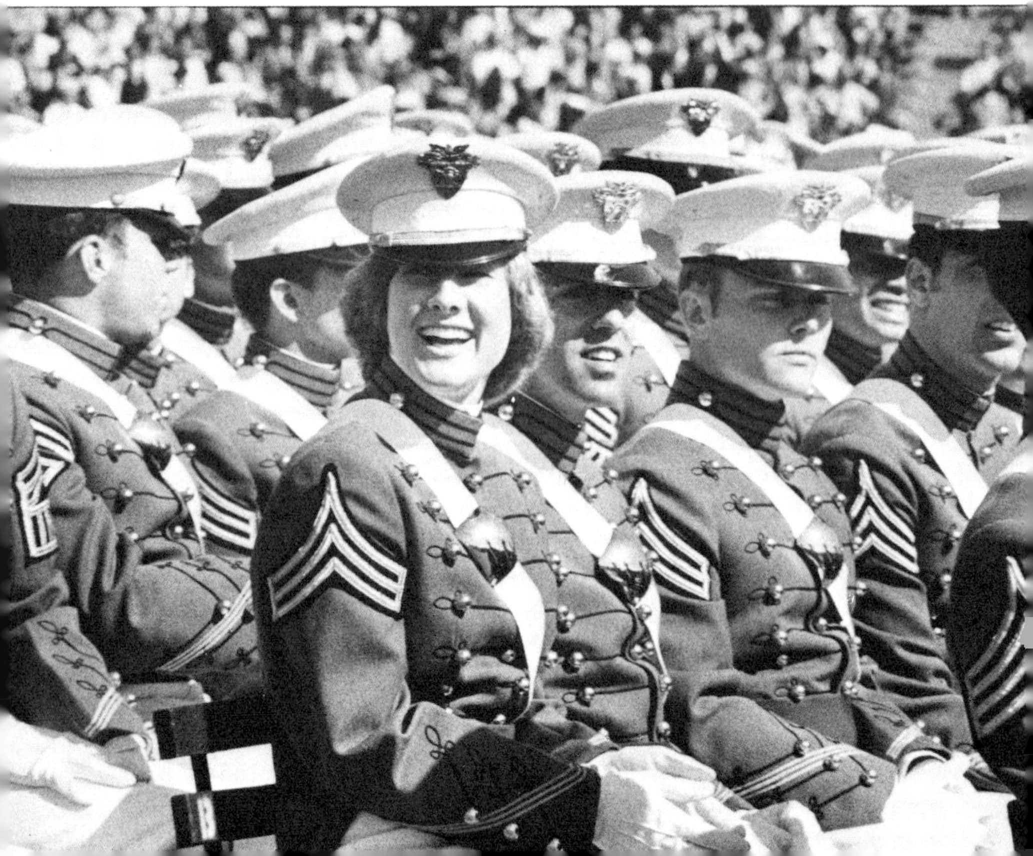

(Above) Midshipmen at the U.S. Naval Academy
in Annapolis, Maryland, during review

(Facing page, top) A young Marine lieutenant poses
in front of his F/A-18 Hornet attack jet
at the U.S. Marine Corps Air Base
in El Toro, California.

(Bottom) This photo was taken at West Point
Military Academy during graduation exercises
in 1980. It was the first Academy graduation
class that included women.

Maryland, for the Navy and Marine Corps; the United States Air Force Academy, Colorado Springs, Colorado; and the United States Coast Guard Academy, New London, Connecticut. Each year about 11 percent of the military's new officers are graduates of these academies. Competition for acceptance is keen, and all but the Coast Guard require a nomination in order to be considered for admission. In most cases nominations are sought from one of the U.S. senators or representatives in a prospective candidate's state. The recommended time to apply for a nomination is in the spring of your junior year in high school. You do not have to know the senator or representative personally to request a nomination.

In addition to senators and congressmen, nominations can come from several other sources, including the vice president of the United States and the secretaries of each branch of military service. Candidates nominated by the secretary of the army, for example, consist of the following six categories: those nominated by the president of the United States (100 nominees); enlisted members of the Regular Army (85); sons and daughters of deceased or totally disabled veterans (20); students from honor military and naval schools and ROTC programs (20); and sons and daughters of persons awarded the Medal of Honor (unlimited). For full information about nomination sources, write to the director of admissions at the military academy of your choice. Also, it is advisable to request nominations from as many sources as possible because of the intense competition.

The requirements for admission to the Army's military academy at West Point are typical of the other service academies. For example, you must be a U.S. citizen and at least seventeen years old but not yet twenty-two on July 1 of the year you wish to enter. Also, you must be unmarried. In addition to completing a physical aptitude test and medical examination, you must take either the American College Testing Assessment Program (ACT) examination or the College Board Admission Testing Program Scholastic Aptitude Test (SAT). The higher your score, the better your chances. Demonstration of leadership potential and physical skills is also important. For this reason, your participation in athletics and school, civic, and church activities will be considered along with your test results.

Each academy offers a four-year program of study leading to a bachelor of science degree. Tuition is free and so are room, board, and medical care. There is also a monthly allowance. When you graduate and receive your commission you are obligated to serve in active duty for at least six years.

★ OFFICER TRAINING WHILE IN COLLEGE (ROTC) ★

If you meet the requirements and qualifications, you can also train to become an officer while attending a public or private college or university through Reserve Officers Training Corps (ROTC) programs conducted by the Army, Navy (including Marine Corps), Air Force, and Marine Corps. These programs are conducted at more than 1,400 U.S. colleges and universities. Depending on the branch of service and the option selected, students train for two, three, or four years.

For example, the Army ROTC program is divided into two parts: the Basic Course and the Advanced Course. The Basic Course covers the first two years of college, the freshman and sophomore years. If, during that period, you decide that a military career is not for you, you can withdraw from the program with no obligation for military service. Those who continue in their junior and senior years enroll in the Advanced Course. They receive uniforms, military science text-

ROTC land navigation exercise

books, and a subsistence allowance of up to $1,000 a year. They also participate in a six-week summer training program between their junior and senior years. (A separate six-week summer training program between the sophomore and junior years is available for students who didn't take the basic course but want to enter the advanced course.)

Scholarships are an important advantage in all ROTC programs. Awarded on a competitive basis, they provide funds for tuition, textbooks, supplies and equipment, laboratory fees, and other educational expenses. Once you have been accepted into an ROTC program, you may apply for two-, three-, and four-year scholarships.

Students in ROTC programs, in addition to meeting regular college requirements, drill several hours each week and receive instruction in military courses. When they graduate from college, they are commissioned as officers and either go on active duty or become members of Reserve or National Guard units. Many of the military's new officers each year, about 37 percent, come through ROTC programs.

★ AFTER GRADUATION FROM COLLEGE ★

The second largest number of new officers each year, 30 percent, come from programs offered to college graduates with no prior military training. There are two designations for this program, depending on the branch of service: Officer Candidate School (OCS) and Officer Training School (OTS). After graduation from college, young men and women who meet the requirements join the military as enlisted personnel while receiving OCS or OTS training, which can last up to twenty weeks. They are then commissioned as officers and obligated to serve four years of active duty.

All newly commissioned officers in these programs go through a period of initial training to familiarize them with the branch of the military they will be serving. They also receive training at schools devoted to their particular job specialty. This part of their training may last from several months to more than a year. For example, after completing Officers Candidate School officers in the Navy's nuclear power program go to Nuclear Power School in Orlando, Florida, for twenty-four weeks, then to a nuclear-power training unit for twenty-six weeks, then to either the Submarine Officer Basic Course for thirteen weeks or to the Surface Warfare Officer School for seventeen weeks before being assigned aboard a nuclear-powered vessel. Average total training time: sixty-five weeks or about one year and three months.

★ DIRECT APPOINTMENTS FOR PROFESSIONALS ★ AND OPPORTUNITIES FOR ENLISTEES

Those professionals who are fully qualified in the medical, legal, engineering, and religious fields may apply for direct appointments as officers. They receive only minimum military training and have a service obligation of two years. A similar program is offered to students in professional schools who receive scholarship assistance in return for several years of military service. About 13 percent of each year's new officers come from these programs. Another 9 percent come from programs that permit enlisted personnel to earn commissions as officers.

Whatever the pathway happens to be that leads to commissioning as an officer, certain basics are emphasized in officer training, including the following:

- ★ An officer's role and responsibilities
- ★ Military laws and regulations
- ★ Service traditions

★ Military customs and courtesies
★ Leadership
★ Career development
★ Military science
★ Administrative procedures

★ TRAINING IN A CAREER SPECIALTY ★

Once an officer receives his or her commission, the next step is training in the career specialty selected. This can last from several weeks to two years, depending on the specialty. Because officers are the leaders in the military, they are expected to develop a broad knowledge of the areas they might command. For instance, suppose you want to become a supply officer. To be considered competent in this specialty you must understand the entire supply system, from contracting to warehouse management to one-day command supply operations for an entire base. For this reason, as a supply officer you will be assigned during your military career to several different jobs, all related to supply management. In preparation for advancement to higher rank and greater responsibilities, you will receive training in leadership, writing, and management skills.

★ CONTINUING EDUCATION ★

Through continuing education programs in each of the services, officers can increase their knowledge and earn advanced degrees in military science, technical subjects related to their career specialties, and management techniques, as well as other subjects in which they have an interest. Educational institutions operated by the services, such as the Naval Postgraduate School and the Air Force Institute of Technology, offer advanced-degree programs through correspondence

Army officers study tank tactics
at Fort Knox, Kentucky.

courses as well as through in-residence programs. In addition, up to 75 percent of tuition costs at public and private colleges and universities are paid for enrollment in night school or correspondence courses. Occasionally, officers are selected to attend graduate-degree programs full-time, with all costs paid, as well as their salaries.

★ DUTY ASSIGNMENTS ★

Once job training is completed, officers are assigned to a military base or ship for duty in a specific job. Each assignment can last from two to four years, depending on needs for a particular specialty and other factors. Later assignments are governed to some extent by need and job performance as well as by officer preferences. Travel is part of a military career. There are hundreds of military bases in the U.S. and countries around the world. The time spent at an Army base overseas can be up to five years, while at bases in the continental U.S. the average time, or tour, of duty is two years. However, you may request permission to stay on at a particular base if there is no need to transfer you to another.

In the Navy, the amount of sea duty versus land duty varies according to the job specialty. It might be two years on land and two years at sea (with stops at various ports and naval installations as well as leave and vacation time). Sometimes the sea duty can be much longer.

★ PAY AND BENEFITS ★

Officers in all branches of the military are paid according to the same pay scale and receive the same basic benefits (Table 4), which are set by the U.S. Congress and usually include an annual cost-of-living in-

Table 4. Summary of Employment Benefits for Officers

Vacation	Leave time of 30 days per year.
Medical, Dental, and Eye Care	Full medical, hospitalization, dental, and eye care services for officers and most health care costs for family members.
Continuing Education	Voluntary educational programs for undergraduate and graduate degrees or for single courses, including tuition assistance for programs at colleges and universities.
Recreational Programs	Programs include athletics, entertainment, and hobbies: Softball, basketball, football, swimming, tennis, golf, weight training, and other sports Parties, dances, and entertainment Club facilities, snack bars, game rooms, movie theaters, and lounges Active hobby and craft clubs, book and music libraries.
Exchange and Commissary Privileges	Food, goods, and services are available at military stores, generally at lower costs.
Legal Assistance	Many free legal services are available to assist with personal matters.

Source: Department of Defense

crease. In addition to pay, the services either provide many of life's necessities, such as food, clothing, and housing, or pay monthly allowances for them. Promotions are based on job performance, leadership ability, years of service, and time in present pay grade. However, the number of officers at advanced pay grades is limited by Congress, and therefore the competition at upper grade levels is intense. Summaries of basic pay and employment benefits for officers are shown on the following pages.

As in the case of enlisted personnel, basic pay is based on pay grade and number of years of service. There is also incentive and special pay, which is in addition to basic pay, for certain types of duty such as submarine and flight duty. Hazardous duty provides monthly incentives or additional pay for such activities as parachute jumping, flight-deck duty, and explosives demolition. There is also special pay for sea duty, diving duty, and duty in some foreign countries and in areas subject to hostile fire. Officers in certain occupations, such as doctors, dentists, and veterinarians, also receive special pay.

Many married officers and their families live free of charge in military housing on the base where the officers have been assigned. If you are single or married and live off the base you are entitled to a monthly housing allowance. In 1991 this ranged from $289.80 to $813.90, depending on pay grade and whether the officer had dependents. In 1991 the food allowance for officers living off-base was $129.00 per month. These allowances are not subject to tax as income and therefore represent significant tax savings in addition to their cash value.

Other benefits for officers include health care for them and their dependents, thirty days leave per year, legal assistance in personal matters, commissary/exchange (military store) privileges, recreational programs, and liberal assistance in completing academic goals in the selected career specialty.

★ RETIREMENT AND VETERANS BENEFITS ★

As an officer, if you retire after twenty years of active duty you will receive monthly payments for life that are equivalent to 40 percent of the average basic pay for the last five years of active duty. Those who retire with more than twenty years' service receive higher pay. Other retirement benefits are similar to those for enlisted personnel, including medical care and commissary/exchange privileges. Also, as a veteran you would be entitled to guarantees for home loans, hospitalization, disability, survivor benefits, and educational benefits. You would also be assisted in finding civilian employment.

★ CHOOSING A PROFESSION ★

Ninety-one percent of all officer candidates have either met or agreed to meet the minimum educational requirement of four years of college with a degree in their chosen field. Only 9 percent advance from the enlisted personnel ranks to the officer level, and these candidates are expected to achieve at least an undergraduate college degree or its equivalent as they assume duty assignments as officers. Many officers continue their education while in the service to earn advanced degrees. If you choose to enter college first before you begin your military career, you have a distinct advantage. When you select a major field of study that best suits your abilities and interests, you are choosing a profession that can easily be accommodated in military or civilian life.

While serving in the military you can be certain of job security and steady advancement in rank and pay as long as you meet performance and other professional standards. Your pay will be comparable to civilian jobs at your officer level, and the opportunity to fulfill your potential in your chosen field will always be there.

In the following pages, several military career options are highlighted as examples of the kinds of careers available to officers in the military. Included in each discussion are the education and training requirements, duties and responsibilities, and reference to jobs in civilian life that would be comparable to that military career specialty.

The armed forces has its own judiciary and trains many lawyers. This is a proceeding of the Army Court of Military Review.

★ SPECIALTY: PURCHASING AND ★ CONTRACT MANAGER

If you have a major interest in management and business or public administration, this career specialty may appeal to you. It requires an ability to develop detailed plans, an interest in work involving accuracy and attention to detail, and an interest in developing good negotiating skills.

Each year the military buys billions of dollars' worth of equipment, supplies, and services from private industry. Officers are needed to make certain these purchases meet military specifications and are made at fair prices. As a purchasing and contracting manager you would negotiate, write, and monitor contracts for purchasing equipment, materials, and services. Here's a more detailed summary of what you would be expected to do:

★ Review requests for supplies and services to make sure they are complete and accurate
★ Prepare bid invitations or requests for proposals for contracts with civilian firms, which specify the type, amount, price, and delivery date for supplies or services
★ Review bids or proposals and award jobs
★ Prepare formal contracts, specifying all terms and conditions
★ Review work to make sure that it meets the requirements of contracts

An officer selected for this profession is normally required to have a four-year college degree. Once you are commissioned, your initial job training will consist of between three and ten weeks of classroom instruction in purchasing and accounting procedures, use of computers in contract administration, and supply and financial management. There are about 5,420 purchasing and contract managers in the military and a need for 310 new managers each year. Officers in this specialty work with and advise commanders on contract proposals, eventually moving up to senior management and command positions.

In civilian life, your professional opportunities would lie with a wide variety of employers, including engineering, manufacturing, and construction firms. Comparable civilian job titles would be procurement services manager, purchasing director, supply manager, and material control manager.

★ SPECIALTY: SOCIAL WORKER ★

The profession of social worker in the military requires a four-year college degree in social work or related social sciences, and some specialties in this field require a master's degree. The number of social workers in the military is relatively small, about 870, with forty new social workers needed each year. However, the numbers do not reflect the importance of this work, which focuses on improving conditions that cause problems, such as drug and alcohol abuse, racism, and sexism.

Military social workers counsel military personnel and their families, supervise counselors and case workers, and survey military personnel to identify problems and plan solutions. They also plan social action programs in efforts to rehabilitate personnel with serious problems. They conduct research on social problems and programs and organize community activities on military bases.

Social workers, whether military or civilian, must be able to speak clearly and distinctly in discussing problems with clients. They must also want to help others and be sensitive to their needs. An interest in teaching and research is helpful. After commissioning as a social worker officer, you will receive from sixteen to twenty-four weeks of instruction in methods of controlling and dealing with drug and alcohol abuse among military personnel. You will then be assigned to a counseling or assistance center. Advancement opportunities include senior management positions.

In civilian life social workers are employed by hospitals, private human-services organizations, and federal, state, county, and city governments. They sometimes specialize in such fields as family services, child welfare, or medical services. Some become social group workers, medical social workers, psychiatric social workers, or social welfare administrators.

★ SPECIALTY: AIR-TRAFFIC-CONTROL MANAGER ★

It helps to have a four-year college degree to qualify for this specialty. Before you can begin duties as an air-traffic-control manager, you must also pass the demanding physical examination required by the Federal Aviation Administration and receive FAA certification, usually during your military training. Depending on your branch of service, you would then work in air-traffic-control towers and centers at airfields and aboard ships. An air-traffic-control center often has several sections, one to give takeoff and landing instructions, another to give ground instructions, and a third to track planes in flight.

As an air-traffic-control manager you would be responsible for some or all of the following duties:

★ Plan work schedules for air-traffic controllers
★ Evaluate job performance of controllers
★ Manage air-traffic-control center operations to ensure safe and efficient flights
★ Inspect control-center facilities and equipment

★ Direct tests of radar equipment and controller procedures
★ Investigate and find solutions to problems in control-center operations
★ Control air traffic using radar and radios
★ Direct training for air-traffic controllers

Good background for this profession would include studies in aeronautical engineering, computer science, and liberal arts. Also helpful are a demonstrated interest in work requiring accuracy and attention to detail, an ability to remain calm in stressful situations, decisiveness, and an ability to manage according to strict standards. Training of from six to eleven weeks consists of classroom instruction in air-traffic-control management, operational procedures, communications and radar procedures, aircraft recognition, and procedures for takeoff, landing, and ground control. There are about 1,250 air-traffic-control managers in the military, and about ninety new managers are needed each year.

★ SPECIALTY: LIFE SCIENTIST ★

Life scientists in the military, just as their counterparts do in civilian life, study the biology and chemistry of living organisms, such as harmful pests and bacteria, to find ways to protect people against illness or infection. They also study human and animal diseases to understand causes and find treatments. About 890 life scientists in the military perform these services, and about eighty new life scientists are needed each year to replace those who have left the military and returned to civilian life.

Some or all of the following duties are performed by life scientists in the military:

★ Study bacteria and parasites to determine how they invade and affect humans or animals
★ Study the effects of drugs, chemicals, and gases on organisms
★ Study ways of protecting from disease through immunization
★ Direct blood banks and study blood chemistry
★ Study the effects of aerospace flight, temperature, and movement on human physiology
★ Study food storage and handling methods
★ Study ways of keeping bases and ships free from pests
★ Conduct experiments and write up the technical reports

To qualify for an officer's commission in this profession you would need a four-year college degree with studies that include biochemistry, biology, microbiology, and pharmacology. You should be able to demonstrate an interest in scientific work that involves mathematics, chemistry, and biology, and an ability to express ideas clearly and concisely.

As a life scientist you would work in a medical, clinical, or research laboratory. Occasionally you would also work outdoors while conducting field work on land or aboard ship, depending on your branch of service. In your initial duty assignment you would conduct research under the direction of more experienced scientists. As you advance in this profession to higher rank and pay and greater responsibilities, eventually you may manage your own research projects and direct other officers. There is a potential for many senior management positions in the health research field, among them director of a research lab.

In civilian life, life scientists work for universities, government agencies, medical laboratories, blood banks, pharmaceutical firms, and chemical companies. Among the comparable civilian job titles are biochemist, biologist, entomologist, immunologist, medical technologist, pharmacologist, physiologist, and toxicologist, depending on the area in which the life scientist is working as well as the research project.

★ SPECIALTY: MISSILE-SYSTEM OFFICER ★

Among the combat specialties in all five branches of military service, none is more important than that filled by the missile-system officer. He or she is responsible for directing missile crews as they target, launch, test, and maintain ballistic missiles. These powerful weapons travel thousands of miles to their targets. They are fired from underground silos, submarines, and land-based launchers. Among the specific duties of the missile-system officer are the following:

★ Stand watch over members of missile launch crews
★ Direct testing and inspection of missile systems
★ Direct missile-maintenance operations
★ Direct early-warning launch training exercises
★ Direct security operations at missile sites
★ Direct the storage and handling of nuclear warheads
★ Direct operation of fail-safe and code-verification systems

A four-year college degree is normally required for this specialty, although in some phases a master's degree in management is preferred. Studies in engineering, physics, computer science, and business or public administration are helpful. So are the abilities to motivate and lead others, to remain calm in stressful situations, and to learn and precisely follow complex procedures.

Training for this profession consists of twelve to nineteen weeks of classroom instruction and training on simulated missile systems. You will be trained in missile targeting, security and code authentication, launch operations, and maintenance programs. There are about 5,280 missile-system officers in the military, and 440 new officers are needed annually. As you advance in this specialty you will manage one or more divisions at a missile site, eventually advancing to senior management and command positions either in missile operations or in other service areas.

FACING THE REALITIES OF MILITARY LIFE

SIX

The Guidance Office at your high school probably has a good supply of recruitment literature from the Department of Defense, including current editions of *Military Career Paths* and *Military Career Guide*. Both publications are useful in providing general information about military life and job specialties available to those young men and women who qualify, either as enlisted personnel or officers. The purpose of these and other military recruitment publications is to interest you in taking the military career option.

There are distinct advantages for those who can adapt to the military routine and responsibilities. This discussion would not be a complete or true picture, however, unless it also detailed some of the disadvantages and some of the pitfalls to avoid.

★ ADJUSTMENTS CAN BE CHALLENGING ★

Being in the military requires a certain amount of adjustment, and Sergeant Marshall Griffin notes that a major adjustment for him "was following orders. As a civilian you're given 'orders' on what needs to be accomplished on the job. The environment can be

When speaking to recruiters and other military representatives, try to get all the facts. Your decision to enter the military should be based on reality, not on "hype."

much more difficult and challenging in the Army. Being in a signal branch of the Army, our main objective was to install, operate, and maintain communication. On one field exercise in Germany, near Bad Kreuznach, in the winter of 1986 we were putting up tents around nine o'clock at night. It was dark, cold, and chow had not arrived. I was cold and hungry and wondering if I'd made a big mistake. I got out of my sleeping bag the next morning to find my toothpaste and deodorant frozen, along with my washcloth, which was in a small, brown, frozen ball. Sleeping in a tent in the middle of a cold German winter was a big adjustment—but also a challenge."

He also recalls that getting used to living in a barracks was another adjustment he had to make. "In Germany we had three-man rooms with personal areas about 8 feet by 10 feet. We slept on bunk beds. Everyone shared the same bathroom [the Army calls it a latrine] and one washer and dryer. By work-call formation everyday, Monday through Friday, usually at 8:30 a.m. [0830], personal and common areas had to be ready for inspection."

The emphasis on physical conditioning can be another difficult adjustment. "In Germany we had PT [physical training] at 6:00 a.m. [0600] everyday. This usually consisted of stretching, warm-up exercises, followed by push-ups and a run, usually between 2 and 4 miles. In Alaska we run outside all winter. More often than not, temperatures are below zero, especially with the chill factor. We are issued headgear called balaclavas to keep our heads and faces warm. You finish a run and you actually have little ice balls on your eyebrows and eyelashes. Your balaclava is covered with frost. They say it gets cold enough at Fort Wainwright in the interior of Alaska that if you throw a cup of coffee in the air, it will freeze before it hits the ground.

"I was at Fort Hood, Texas, from May of 1988 to May of 1990. It was scorching in the summer. Fire ants were a big nuisance. You would go to sleep in the tent at night, and when you got up the next day your fingers would be swollen from the bites. It was so hot you couldn't sleep in your sleeping bag. You couldn't escape them; at least I couldn't.

"I was single at the time, and Christmas and holidays were sometimes difficult. Mail from home was really appreciated. Those soldiers who were married invited me over for holiday dinners. When I went overseas to duty in Germany, the Army seemed more like a family. I think being in a foreign country helps bond everyone more together, and yet the same kind of feeling holds true in Alaska."

★ THE MARRIED ENLISTED MAN ★

"I got married June 25, 1988, while I was stationed at Fort Hood, Texas," Sergeant Griffin adds, pointing out that "There were many changes. I no longer had to live in the barracks. I didn't have to worry about keeping common areas and personal areas inspection-ready." He also recalls some of the paper work involved. "There is quite a bit of paper work to fill out for your spouse once you become married. You can choose for your wife or other family member to receive insurance money, usually $50,000, if you are killed while on active duty. If you are authorized to live off-post, the Army gives you a basic allowance for quarters [BAQ] to be used for housing. A separate amount called a variable housing allowance [VHA] is given to soldiers in areas where there is a higher cost of living. In Alaska that amounts to $499 a month for my pay grade."

All of these changes involved paper work, and so did certain legal requirements. "Wills and power-ofattorney documents have to be prepared so that my interests and my wife's interests will be protected when I am deployed in time of war or other military action. Also, I had to put my wife's name on the checking account so she would have access to it."

★ SOME DRAWBACKS FROM AN OFFICER'S ★ POINT OF VIEW

Speaking just before the U.S. became involved in the Persian Gulf War in 1991, Captain Patrick J. Eberhart was quick to point out that the chief disadvantage is the potential for war. He also mentioned some others. "Dealing with bureaucracies and an occasional difficult leader are some other disadvantages. However, many disadvantages are minimized if you accept the overall decision to make the military a career. The average human being is a very flexible, adaptable creature. Once you learn the rules of a system/business, it becomes easier to accept. I think in today's society the biggest adjustment that young men and women face is the discipline that the military requires.

"Many soldiers love discipline and appreciate rules, regulations, and known quantities. However, a lot of middle-class kids aren't given guidelines when growing up because their parents attempt to 'let them make their own decisions.' In the same light, a lot of kids coming from poor or underclass families either do not have both parents to guide them or their parents don't care. In either case the result is the same: kids that want to be given rules, want to do the right thing, and want to better their lot in life.

"An adjustment I had to make was to do the right thing because it was the 'right thing' and not because someone else is checking on me or because someone else wants it done. Establishing your personal standards of living and work is not as easy as it sounds. A lot of growing up has to be done to achieve this level of maturity."

"The Army is not operated as it appears on television or in the movies," Captain Eberhart stresses. "A lot of the glamour and excitement depicted seldom happens, and glamour and excitement are the exception, not the rule. For some people the rules/orders/discipline are too much to handle, and so is the idea that once you sign on the dotted line you 'belong to Uncle Sam.' That is not always compatible with modern American living standards and life-styles."

There are other adjustments if you serve in the military and are married, whether officer or enlisted man or woman. Captain Eberhart had been in the Army almost four years before he got married. At the time his wife was also in the military. "When she was," Captain Eberhart says, "there were advantages and disadvantages. Some of the advantages have continued. For example, she understands the military lifestyle, the commitment to travel, time apart, deployments and other hardships. In time of war or conflict there is always the possibility that both husband and wife could be deployed to a combat area [there were instances of this during the Persian Gulf War]. If there are children this could cause hardships in taking care of the children properly and taking care of the normal operations of running a household.

"There is also the possibility of being separated for long periods of time from your spouse. The military attempts to station married servicemembers at the same location, but this is not always possible due to mission/manning goals. However, the major adjustment for most married couples is learning how to adjust to being away from 'the nest' or adapting to the military's transient existence, with moves to new bases or posts every three or four years, either in the U.S. or in a foreign country."

★ FROM MILITARY TO CIVILIAN LIFE ★

Making the transition from military to civilian life, especially after many years of military service, can be difficult and far less rewarding than you may have been led to suppose. Consider this example from the enlisted-personnel side of the coin: Dwight Brantley, thirty-five years old when he left military service, had attained the rank of sergeant and been a cook at Walter Reed Army Medical Center in Washington, D.C. When he left the Army he got a job at the nearby Children's Hospital National Medical Center, also as a cook. However, his employer told him he would not be able to advance in his job until he took some civilian courses in dietetics, even though he had been trained in dietetics when he was in the Army. As reported in the April 15, 1991, issue of *Forbes* magazine, Brantley's employer, Marriott Corporation, might start an ex-serviceman or ex-servicewoman who had been earning the equivalent of $32,000 while running a military cafeteria at the much lower salary of $20,000 as a first-line supervisor.

The same jolt awaits many newly retired officers who seek civilian employment, according to Douglas Carter, director of placement for the Retired Officers Association. A retired Air Force colonel himself, Carter reported that colonels who had been earning the equivalent of $75,000 a year in pay and tax-free allowances could expect only $40,000 in their first civilian jobs.

Officers of lower rank and fewer years of service fare much better. According to Janet Novack, author of the *Forbes* article, "Some companies regularly tap the pool of 8,000 or so junior officers who leave the military annually in their mid- to late twenties. These employers find the young officers hustle and have unusual maturity for their age. Pizza Hut starts junior officers alongside M.B.A.s [those with a master's degree in business administration] in its fast-track training program. Kimberly-Clark draws half its consumer products production management trainees from the military. And a slew of health care companies, including Johnson & Johnson, Abbott Laboratories, and Baxter International, find junior officers make great salespeople."

Also faring better are those ex-servicemen, former enlisted men and women as well as officers, whose job specialties can be put to direct use in civilian jobs, such as telecommunications and electronics repair. Those in military job specialties in which there is the potential hazard of learning bureaucratic bad habits may not do as well financially in the initial transition from military to civilian life. Most servicemen who join the civilian work force, however, are praised for their work ethic of discipline and loyalty.

APPENDIX A:
SAMPLE ASVAB TEST QUESTIONS

The Armed Services Vocational Aptitude Battery test has been designed by the U.S. Department of Defense with two purposes in mind. One is to help schools assist students in identifying their aptitudes and developing future educational and career plans. The other is to assist the military in identifying those best qualified for a variety of military career specialties. Following are some sample ASVAB test questions (and answers) to give you an idea of the range of questions asked.

★ GENERAL SCIENCE ★

This test consists of 25 questions encompassing both physical and biological science. Each question is followed by four alternatives from which you are to select the correct answer and blacken the corresponding space on your answer sheet.

The sample below has already been answered for you. Be sure you understand it. Then answer the two questions following it as best you can.

SAMPLE QUESTION

Water is an example of a

A. crystal.
B. solid.
C. gas.
D. liquid.

D is the correct answer.

Questions

1. An eclipse of the sun throws the shadow of the

   1-A. moon on the sun.
   1-B. moon on the earth.
   1-C. earth on the sun.
   1-D. earth on the moon.

   B is the correct answer.

2. Substances which hasten chemical reaction time without themselves undergoing change are called

   2-A. buffers.
   2-B. colloids.
   2-C. reducers.
   2-D. catalysts.

   D is the correct answer.

★ PARAGRAPH COMPREHENSION ★

This test contains 15 items measuring your ability to obtain information from written passages. In this section you will find one or more paragraphs of reading material followed by incomplete statements or questions. You are to read the paragraph(s) and select one of the lettered choices which best completes the statement or answers the question.

Read the sample below carefully and choose the best answer to complete the paragraph or answer the question. Make sure you understand it. Then answer the two questions following it, blackening the corresponding spaces on your answer sheet.

SAMPLE QUESTION

From a building designer's standpoint, three things that make a home livable are the client, the building site, and the amount of money the client has to spend. **According to the passage, to make a home livable**

A. the prospective piece of land makes little difference.
B. it can be built on any piece of land.
C. the design must fit the owner's income and site.
D. the design must fit the designer's income.

The correct answer is **C**.

★ CODING SPEED ★

This is a test of 84 items to see how quickly and accurately you can find a number in a table. At the top of each section there is a number table or "Key." The key is a group of words with a code number for each word. Each question in the test is a word taken from the key listed above it. From among the possible answers listed for each question, find the one that is the correct code number for that word.

Look at the sample key and answer the five sample questions below. Make sure you understand it. Then answer the 14 questions following it as quickly as you can, blackening the corresponding spaces on your answer sheet.

KEY

green ...2715	man ...3451	salt ...4586
hat ...1413	room ...2864	tree ...5972

SAMPLE QUESTIONS   ANSWERS

	A	B	C	D	E
1. room	1413	2715	2864	3541	4586
2. green	2715	2864	3451	4586	5972
3. tree	1413	2715	3451	4586	5972
4. hat	1413	2715	3451	4586	5972
5. room	1413	2864	3451	4586	5972

The correct answers are **1-C, 2-A, 3-E, 4-A, 5-B.**

★ AUTO & SHOP INFORMATION ★

This test has 25 questions about automobiles, shop practices, and the use of tools. Pick the best answer for each question.

The sample question below has already been answered for you. Be sure you understand it. Then answer the questions that follow, blackening the corresponding spaces on your answer sheet.

SAMPLE QUESTION

A chisel is used for

A. prying.
B. cutting.

C. twisting.
D. grinding.

B is the correct answer.

Questions

1. A car uses too much oil when which parts are worn?

   A. pistons.
   B. piston rings.
   C. main bearings.
   D. connecting rods.

   B is the correct answer.

2. The saw shown is used mainly to cut

   A. plywood.
   B. odd-shaped holes in wood.
   C. along the grain of the wood.
   D. across the grain of the wood.

   B is the correct answer.

★ MECHANICAL COMPREHENSION ★

This test contains 25 questions designed to measure your understanding of mechanical principles. Many of the questions use drawings to illustrate specific principles. Each question is followed by four possible answers from which you are to select the correct response.

The sample question below has already been answered for you. Make sure you understand it. Then answer the two questions following it as best you can, blackening the corresponding spaces on your answer sheet.

SAMPLE QUESTION

If gear A makes 14 revolutions, gear B will make

A. 21.
B. 17.
C. 14.
D. 9.

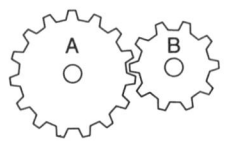

A is the correct answer.

Questions

1. Which post holds up the greater part of the load?

   A. post A.
   B. post B.
   C. both equal.
   D. not clear.

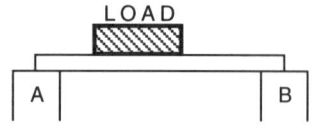

   A is the correct answer.

2. In this arrangement of pulleys, which pulley turns fastest?

   A. A.
   B. B.
   C. C.
   D. D.

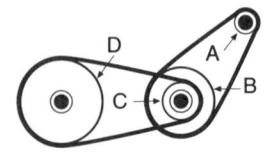

   A is the correct answer.

★ ELECTRONICS INFORMATION ★

This test consists of 20 questions dealing with electricity, radio principles, and electronics. Each question is followed by four possible answers from which you are to select the best response.

The sample question below has already been answered for you. Make sure you understand it. Then answer the two questions following it, blackening the corresponding spaces on your answer sheet.

SAMPLE QUESTION

What does the abbreviation A.C. stand for?

A. additional charge
B. alternating coil
C. alternating current
D. ampere current

C is the correct answer.

Questions
1. Which of the following has the least resistance?

A. wood
B. iron
C. rubber
D. silver

D is the correct answer.

2. In the schematic vacuum tube illustrated, the cathode is element

A. A
B. B
C. C
D. D

D is the correct answer.

APPENDIX B:
SPECIALTIES FOR ENLISTED MEN AND WOMEN

The following is a list of 134 occupations open to enlisted men and women in the five branches of military service—Army, Navy, Air Force, Marine Corps, and Coast Guard. *This list is by no means complete, but it will give you a good idea of the variety of job opportunities available.*

Combat Specialties

Artillery crew members
Combat engineers
Infantrymen
Special operations forces
Tank crew members

Human Services

Caseworkers and counselors
Recreation specialists
Religious program specialists

Media and Public Affairs

Audiovisual production specialists
Graphic designers and illustrators
Interpreters and translators
Motion-picture-camera operators
Musicians
Photographers
Radio and television announcers
Reporters and newswriters

Health Care

Cardiopulmonary and EEG technicians
Dental specialists
Medical laboratory technicians
Medical record technicians
Medical service technicians
Nursing technicians
Occupational-therapy specialists
Operating-room technicians
Optometric technicians
Orthopedic technicians
Orthotic specialists
Pharmacy technicians
Physical-therapy specialists
Radiologic (X-ray) technicians
Respiratory therapists

Engineering, Science, and Other Technical Jobs

Air-traffic controllers
Broadcast and recording technicians
Computer programmers
Computer-systems analysts

Drafters
Emergency management specialists
Environmental health specialists
Fuel and chemical laboratory technicians
Intelligence specialists
Legal technicians
Mapping technicians
Nondestructive testers
Radar and sonar operators
Radio-intelligence operators
Radio operators
Space-systems specialists
Surveying technicians
Weather observers

Administration

Accounting specialists
Administrative-support specialists
Computer operators
Court reporters
Data-entry specialists
Dispatchers
Flight-operations specialists
Lodging specialists
Maintenance data analysts
Payroll specialists
Personnel specialists
Postal specialists
Recruiting specialists

(Facing page) Air Force technician works on a solar-powered microwave antenna system.

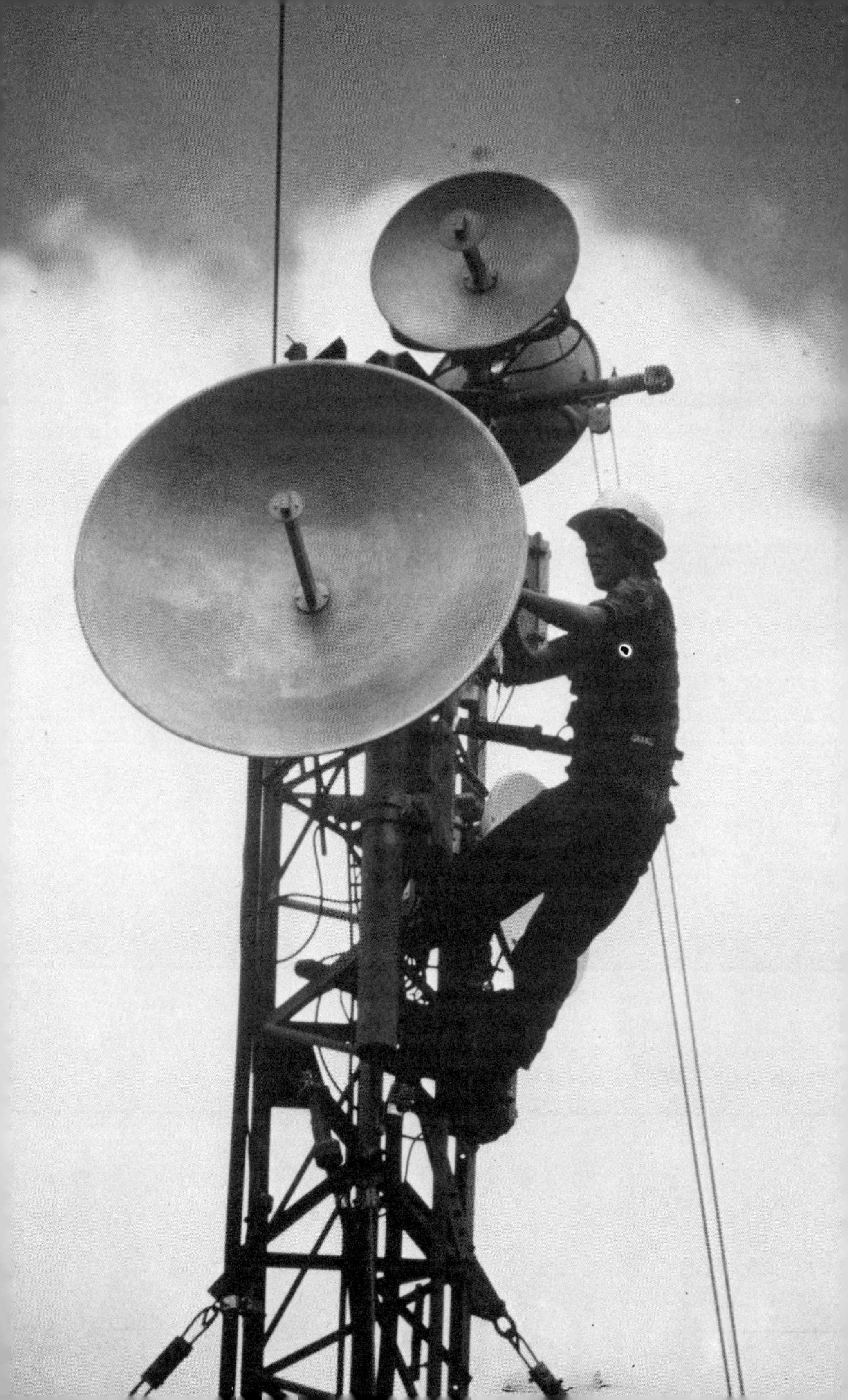

Army soldier using a surveying transit

Sales and stock specialists
Secretaries and stenographers
Shipping and receiving specialists
Stock and inventory specialists
Telephone operators
Teletype operators
Trainers
Transportation specialists

Services

Barbers
Corrections specialists
Detectives
Firefighters
Food-service specialists
Military police

Vehicle and Machinery Mechanics

Aircraft mechanics
Automobile mechanics
Automotive body repairers
Drivers
Engine mechanics
Heating and cooling mechanics
Heavy-equipment mechanics
Marine-engine mechanics
Office-machine repairers
Powerhouse mechanics
Riggers

Electronic and Electrical Equipment Repairers

Aircraft electricians
Data-processing-equipment repairers

Electrical-products repairers
Electronic-instrument repairers
Electronic-weapons-systems repairers
Line installers and repairers
Ordnance mechanics
Photographic equipment repairers
Power-plant electricians
Precision-instrument repairers
Radar- and sonar-equipment repairers
Radio-equipment repairers
Ship electricians
Telephone technicians
Teletype repairers

——————— **Construction Trades** ———————

Blasting specialists
Bricklayers and concrete masons
Building electricians
Carpenters
Ironworkers
Paving-equipment operators
Plumbers and pipe fitters
Well drillers

——————— **Machine Operators and Precision Workers** ———————

Boiler technicians
Clothing and fabric repairers
Compressed-gas technicians
Dental laboratory technicians
Machinists
Opticians
Photoprocessing specialists
Power-plant operators
Printing specialists

A member of the 62nd Transportation Company,
U.S. Army, drives an M-915 14-ton tractor truck.

Sheet-metal workers
Shipfitters
Survival-equipment specialists
Water- and sewage-treatment-plant operators
Welders

— **Transportation and Material Handling** —

Aircraft launch and recovery specialists
Air crew members
Boat operators
Cargo specialists
Construction-equipment operators
Flight engineers
Petroleum supply specialists
Quartermasters
Seamen
Truck drivers

APPENDIX C:
SPECIALTIES FOR OFFICERS

The following list of officer occupations shows what a broad range of career opportunities the military offers to its officer candidates.

Combat Specialties

Artillery officers
Infantry officers
Missile-system officers
Special-operations officers
Tank officers

Executive, Administrative, and Managerial

Accountants and auditors
Attachés
Communications managers
Data-processing managers
Education and training directors
Emergency management officers
Financial managers
Food-service managers

Health-services administrators
Management analysts
Personnel managers
Postal directors
Purchasing and contracting managers
Recreation directors
Recruiting managers
Store managers
Supply and warehousing managers
Teachers and instructors
Transportation maintenance managers
Transportation managers

Human Services

Chaplains
Social workers

Media and Public Affairs

Audiovisual production directors
Band managers
Public-information officers

Health Diagnosing and Treatment

Dentists
Optometrists
Physicians and surgeons
Podiatrists
Psychologists
Veterinarians

Health Care

Dietitians
Environmental-health officers

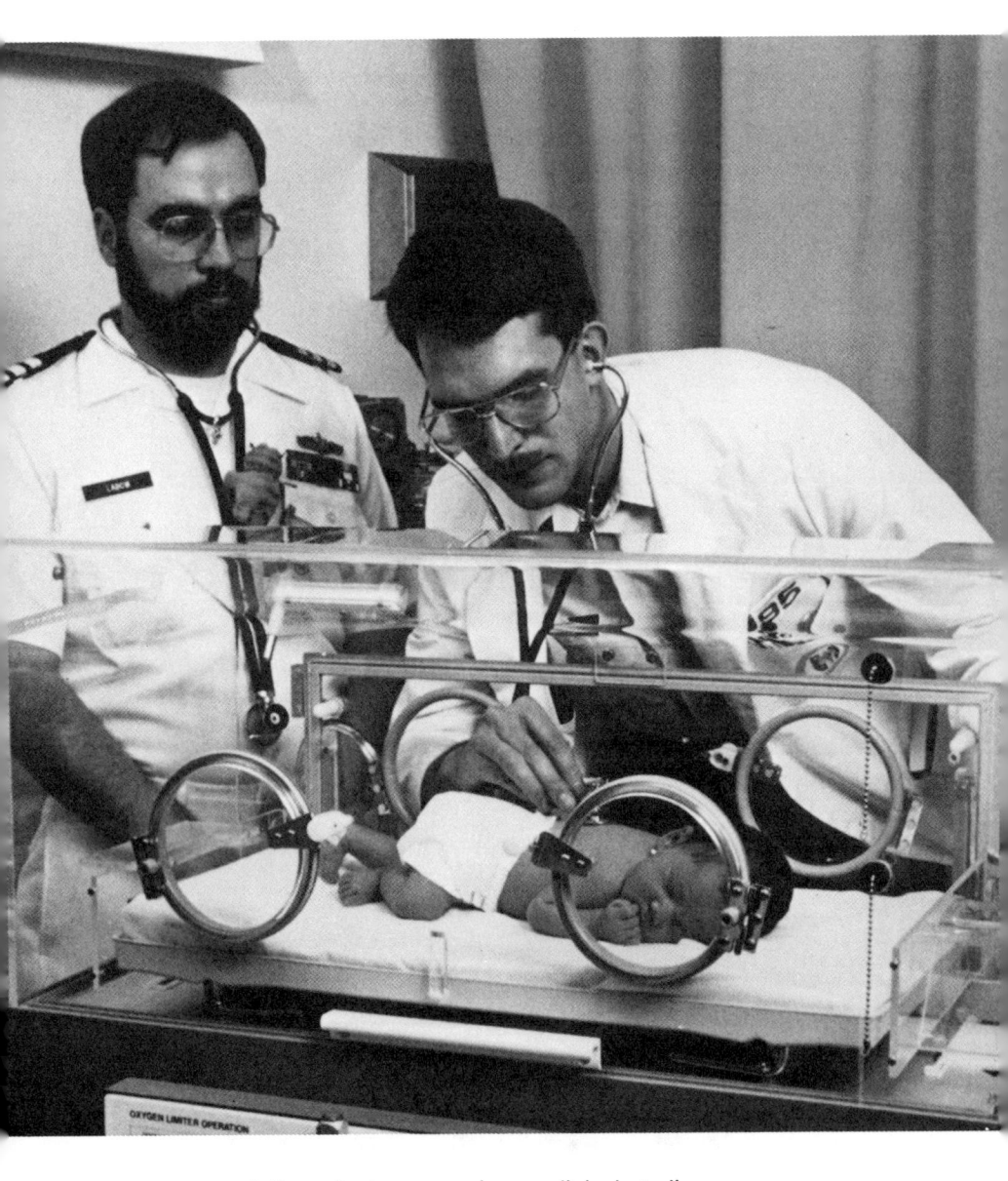

A Navy doctor supervises a clinical studies student as he examines a baby at the Uniformed Services University of the Health Sciences.

An Air Force captain works with a laser.

Occupational therapists
Pharmacists
Physical therapists
Physician assistants
Registered nurses
Speech therapists

Engineering, Science, and Other Technicians

Aerospace engineers
Air-traffic-control managers
Chemists
Civil engineers
Computer-systems-development officers
Computer-systems engineers
Electrical and electronic engineers
Industrial engineers
Intelligence officers
Lawyers
Life scientists
Marine engineers
Meteorologists
Nuclear engineers
Oceanographers
Operations analysts
Physicists
Space-operations officers
Surveying and mapping managers

Service Occupations

Law-enforcement directors
Security officers
Special agents

Transportation

Airplane navigators
Airplane pilots
Helicopter pilots
Ship and submarine officers
Ship engineers

FOR FURTHER READING

Air Force Times, *Army Times*, and *Navy Times*, independent weekly newspapers, published by the *Times-Journal*, 6883 Commercial Drive, Springfield, Virginia 22159-0160, copies available in recruiting offices and in libraries on military bases or by subscription

Intel Staff, *Military Handbook, Nineteen-Eighty-Eight*, Intel Corporation, 1988

Karsten, Peter, Editor, *Military in America: From the Colonial Era to the Present*, Free Press, 1980

Military Career Guide, Employment and Training Opportunities in the Military, updated periodically, copies usually available in high school guidance offices, U.S. Department of Defense, Washington, D.C.

Military Career Paths, Career Progression Patterns for Selected Occupations from the *Military Career Guide*, U.S. Department of Defense, Washington, D.C.

Schwan, Fred, and Pick, Albert, Editors, *Military Vignettes*, BNR Press, 1986

Scowcroft, Brent, *Military Service in the United States*, American Assembly, 1982

INDEX

Italicized page numbers refer to photographs.

Advanced Electronics Training Program, 70
Advanced Individual Training (AIT) schools, 62
Air Force, 26, 28, 64–66
Air Force Academy, 76
Air-traffic-control managers, 90–91
Aptitude Index Program, 28
Armed Services Vocational Aptitude Battery (ASVAB) test, 22, 32, 33–36, 37, 103–9
Army, 22, 24, 57, 61–63
Army Band, 23
Audiovisual production specialists, 43–44

Bradley fighting vehicle, *50*

Civilian Acquired Skills Program, 24

Civilian life following service, 101–2
Coast Guard, 31, 69–70
Coast Guard Academy, 76
College, financing for, 9–10, 16, 57, 69
College Enlistment Program, 31
College Level Examination Program, 66
Communication skills, 15, 21
Community College of the Air Force, 65–66
Computer systems analysts, 44, *45*, 46

Decision-making skills, 16
Delayed Entry Program, 24, 26, 28, 30

Engine mechanics, 46, 47, 48–49
Enlisted persons adjustment to military life, 95, 97–98

application for enlistment, 37
ASVAB test, 22, 32, 35–36, 37, 103–9
benefits of service, 12, 15–17
financial incentives, 57, 60–61
job opportunities, 38–52, 110–18
married life, 98–99
officer commissions for, 80
pay and benefits, 56–57, 61
qualifications for enlistment, 22, 24, 26, 30–31
recruiting process, 37–38, 95
training for, 61–70
Enlistment Option Program, 30–31
Extension Course Institute (ECI), 66

GI Bill, 57
Guaranteed Training Enlistment Program, 28

Infantrymen, 49, 51–52

Journalism school, 17

Life scientists, 91–93

Mail from home, 98
Marine Corps, 28, 30–31, 66, 68–69

Marine Corps Basic Skills Education Program, 68
Medical laboratory technicians, 39, 42, 43
Meritorious Promotion System, 68
Military academies, 73, 74, 75, 76–77
Military occupational specialties (MOS), 15, 30–31, 68
Missile-system officers, 93–94

Naval Academy, 73, 75, 76
Navy, 24, 26, 63–64, 80
  sea duty, 83
Navy Campus program, 64
Nuclear Power School, 80

Officer Candidate School (OCS), 19, 79–80
Officers
  benefits of service, 17, 19–21
  career specialties, 73, 81, 86–94, 119–24
  continuing education programs, 81, 83
  drawbacks of officer life, 99–101
  duty assignments, 83
  educational attainments, 19–20
  as executives, 71, 73
  married life, 85, 100–101
  military-academy training, 73, 76–77

pay and benefits, 83–85
professionals, appointments for, 80
retirement benefits, 21, 85–86
ROTC program, 19, 20, 77, 78, 79
Officer Training School (OTS), 19, 79–80
On-call status, 10

Pay periods, 10
Persian Gulf War, *11*, 12, 26, 28, *29*, 100
Physical exams, 38
Physical training, 97
Physician's Assistant Program, 69–70
Progressive Service School Training Program, 62–63
Purchasing managers, 88–89

Quality Enlistment Program, 31

Reserve Officers Training Corps (ROTC), 19, 20, 77, 78, 79

Servicemembers Opportunity Colleges (SOC) system, 68–69
Social workers, 89–90
Student loan "forgiveness" program, 57, 60
Subfarer Program, 64
Survival skills, 16

Travel, 17, 20, 83
Tuition Assistance Program, 69

Underwater Photography Team (UPT), 34

Vacations, 10

West Point Military Academy, 73, 74, 76–77
Women, 30, 53, *54*, 56
Work day, 10

CAMBRIA COUNTY LIBRARY

8 5131 00009662 9   02

SEP 1993

```
355      Dunbar, Robert E.,
D899g    1926-
         Guide to military
           careers
```

CAMBRIA COUNTY LIBRARY
Johnstown, PA 15901

DEMCO